SIDE by SIDE

Plus

BOOK 2A

Life Skills, Standards, & Test Prep

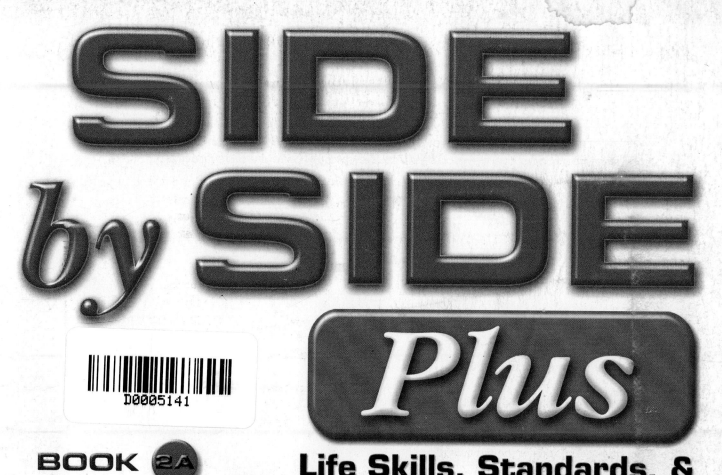

Steven J. Molinsky • Bill Bliss

Illustrated by Richard E. Hill

PEARSON
Longman

Dedicated to Tina Carver with gratitude for her inspiration and
contribution to the development of the original *Side by Side* program.

Steven J. Molinsky
Bill Bliss

Side by Side Plus, Book 2A

Pearson Education, 10 Bank Street, White Plains, NY 10606

Editorial director: *Pam Fishman*
Vice president, director of design and production: *Rhea Banker*
Director of electronic production: *Aliza Greenblatt*
Director of manufacturing: *Patrice Fraccio*
Senior manufacturing manager: *Edith Pullman*
Director of marketing: *Oliva Fernandez*
Production editor: *Diane Cipollone*
Senior digital layout specialists: *Wendy Wolf; Warren Fischbach; Lisa Ghiozzi*
Text design: *Wanda España, Wee Design Group; Wendy Wolf*
Cover design: *Wanda España, Wee Design Group; Warren Fischbach*
Realia creation: *Wendy Wolf; Warren Fischbach*
Image archivist: *Paula Williams*
Illustrations: *Richard E. Hill*
Principal photographer: *Paul I. Tañedo*
Contributing authors: *Laura English, Elizabeth Handley, Meredith Westfall*
Manager, visual research: *Beth Brenzel*
Image permission coordinator: *Angelique Sharps*
Photo researcher: *Teri Stratford*

Additional photos: p.10c Spencer Grant/Photo Researchers, Inc.; p.18a (*center, right*) Valerie Schultz/Merrill Education; p.27 (*left*) David Young-Wolff/PhotoEdit, (*right*) Rudy Von Briel/PhotoEdit; p.28 (*top*) Cosmo Condina/Stone, (*bottom*) David Young Wolff/PhotoEdit, (*center*) Don Smetzer/Stone; p.38c Ariel Skelley/Blend Images/Getty Images; p.48a (*top row, first*) David Mager, (*top row, second*) Lenovo Group Limited, (*top row, third*) Macdaddy/Dreamstime, (*top row, fourth*) Z.Legacy.Images Resource Centers/Epson American, Inc., (*second row, first*) Paul Wilkinson, (*second row, second*) David Mager, (*second row, third*) Don Farrall/Getty Images; p.48b (*left*) Johann Helgason/iStockphoto, (*right*) Shutterstock; p.58a (*top row, third*) William Milner/Shutterstock, (*top row, fourth*) Hrudinin Vasyl/Shutterstock; p.59 (*top*) Courtesy Guinness World Records, Ltd., (*center, left*) Inacio Teixeira/AP/Wide World Photos, (*center, right*) Hugh Sitton/Stone, (*bottom, left*) Chad Ehlers/Stone; p.60 (*top*) Ray Stott/The Image Works, (*center*) Margot Granitsas/The Image Works, (*bottom*) Popperfoto/Archive Photos.

Pearson Longman on the Web
PearsonLongman.com offers online resources for teachers and students.
Access our Companion Websites, our online catalog, and our local offices around the world.
Visit us at pearsonlongman.com.

ISBN 978-0-13-209012-4; 0-13-209012-0

Printed in the United States of America
1 2 3 4 5 6 7 8 9 10 –QWD– 12 11 10 09 08

CONTENTS

Red type indicates new standards-based lessons.

Dear Friends,

Welcome to **Side by Side Plus**—a special edition for adult learners that offers an integrated standards-based and grammar-based approach to language learning!

Flexible Language Proficiency *Plus* Life Skills

The core mission of *Side by Side Plus* is to build students' general language proficiency so they can use English flexibly to meet their varied needs, life circumstances, and goals. We strongly believe that language teachers need to preserve their role as true teachers of language even as we fill our lesson plans with required life-skill content and prepare students for standardized tests. Our program helps you accomplish this through a research-based grammatical sequence and communicative approach in which basic language lessons in each unit lead to standards-based lessons focused on students' life-skill roles in the community, family, school, and at work.

Keys to Promoting Student Persistence and Success

STUDENT-CENTERED LEARNING   The core methodology of *Side by Side Plus* is the guided conversation—a brief, structured dialog that students practice in pairs and then use as a framework to create new conversations. Through this practice, students work together to develop their language skills "side by side." They are not dependent on the teacher for all instruction, and they know how to learn from each other. This student-centered methodology and the text's easy-to-use format enable students to study outside of class with any speaking partner—a family member, a friend or neighbor, a tutor, or a co-worker, even if that person is also an English language learner. If students need to attend class intermittently or "stop out" for a while, they have the skills and text material to continue learning on their own.

MEANINGFUL INSTRUCTION RELEVANT TO STUDENTS' LIVES   Throughout the instructional program, civics topics and tasks connect students to their community, personalization questions apply lesson content to students' life situations, and critical-thinking activities build a community of learners who problem-solve together and share solutions.

EXTENDING LEARNING OUTSIDE THE CLASSROOM   The magazine-style Gazette sections in *Side by Side Plus* provide motivating material for students to use at home. Feature articles, vocabulary enrichment, and other activities reinforce classroom instruction through high-interest material that

students are motivated to use outside of class. A bonus Audio CD offers entertaining radio program-style recordings of key Gazette activities. (See the inside back cover for a description of other media materials and software designed to extend learning through self-study.)

SUFFICIENT PRACTICE + FREQUENT ASSESSMENT = SUCCESS   Students need to experience success as language learners. While other programs "cover" many learning objectives, *Side by Side Plus* offers students carefully-sequenced intensive practice that promotes mastery and the successful application of language skills to daily life. Students can observe their achievement milestones through the program's frequent assessments, including check-up tests and skills checklists in the text and achievement tests in the accompanying workbook.

THE "FUN FACTOR"   We believe that language instruction is most powerful when it is joyful. There is magic in the power of humor, fun, games, and music to encourage students to take risks with their emerging language, to "play" with it, and to allow their personalities to shine through as their language skills increase. We incorporate these elements into our program to motivate students to persist in their language learning not only because they need it, but also because they enjoy it.

MULTILEVEL INSTRUCTION   *Side by Side Plus* provides exceptional resources to support multilevel instruction. The Teacher's Guide includes step-by-step instructions for preparing below-level and at-level students for each lesson and hundreds of multilevel activities for all students, including those above-level. The accompanying Multilevel Activity & Achievement Test Book and CD-ROM offer an array of reproducible multilevel worksheets and activities.

We hope your students enjoy using *Side by Side Plus*. We are confident that these resources will help them persist and succeed through a language learning experience that is effective . . . relevant to their lives . . . and fun!

Steven J. Molinsky
Bill Bliss

Guide to Life Skills, Standards, & Test Prep Features

Side by Side has helped over 25 million students worldwide persist and succeed as language learners. Now, in this special edition for adult learners in standards-based programs, *Side by Side Plus* builds students' general language proficiency *and* helps them apply these skills for success meeting the needs of daily life and work.

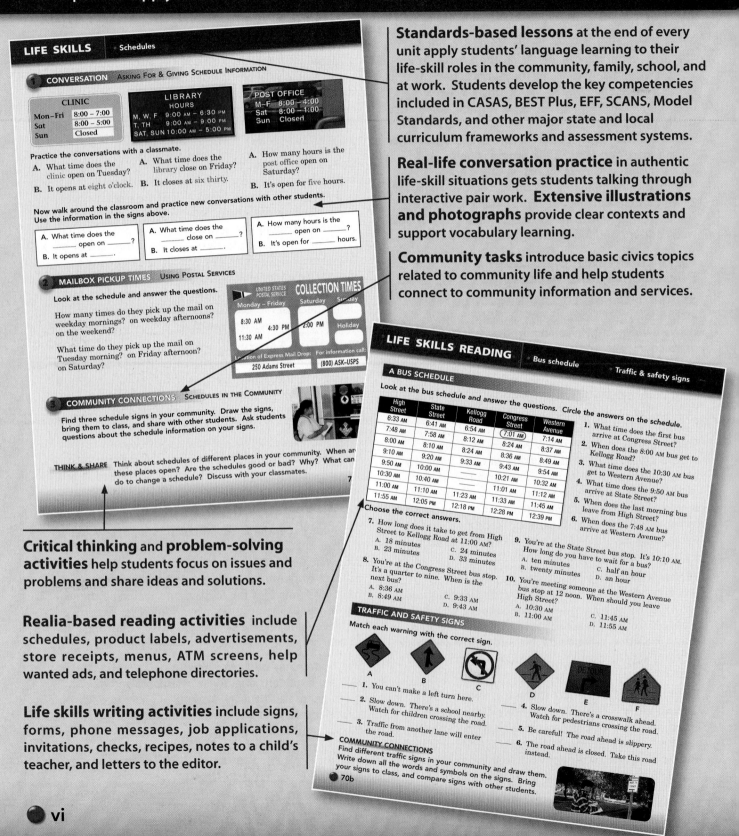

Standards-based lessons at the end of every unit apply students' language learning to their life-skill roles in the community, family, school, and at work. Students develop the key competencies included in CASAS, BEST Plus, EFF, SCANS, Model Standards, and other major state and local curriculum frameworks and assessment systems.

Real-life conversation practice in authentic life-skill situations gets students talking through interactive pair work. **Extensive illustrations and photographs** provide clear contexts and support vocabulary learning.

Community tasks introduce basic civics topics related to community life and help students connect to community information and services.

Critical thinking and **problem-solving activities** help students focus on issues and problems and share ideas and solutions.

Realia-based reading activities include schedules, product labels, advertisements, store receipts, menus, ATM screens, help wanted ads, and telephone directories.

Life skills writing activities include signs, forms, phone messages, job applications, invitations, checks, recipes, notes to a child's teacher, and letters to the editor.

Safe Driving

More than 3.5 million people get hurt in car accidents in the United States each year. Here are some things you can do so that you and your passengers are safe.

Always wear a seat belt. Also, make sure that all the passengers in your car wear their seat belts. Children under the age of five should ride in child safety seats that you attach to the back seat of the car. The center back seat is the safest.

Many accidents happen when cars are in bad condition. Take good care of your car. Check the brakes every week to be sure that you can stop the car when you need to. Keep the windshield clean so you can see the road ahead. Be sure the windshield wipers work in the rain.

Be a careful driver. Pay attention to traffic signs, road conditions, and other drivers. Look before you make a turn or change lanes on the highway. Don't "tailgate"—don't stay too close to the car in front of you. The driver might stop without warning. Be especially careful when the weather is bad. Slow down and use your headlights in the rain, snow, and fog. Pay attention to the speed limit. When

the speed limit is sixty miles an hour, that's the fastest you should drive. On the other hand, don't be a slow driver. Slow drivers can cause accidents.

You can't pay attention to the road when you're tired or busy doing too many things. Don't eat, drink, or talk on your cell phone while you're driving. Don't take any medicine that can make you sleepy before you drive. The label on such medicine usually has the warning "May cause drowsiness." Remember, other drivers are not always as careful as you are. Be prepared for their mistakes. If you are in an accident, the police will ask to see your papers. Always have your license, car registration, and insurance card with you to show to the police.

1. The best place for a child safety seat is ___.
   A. in the front seat
   B. in the back seat next to the door
   C. in the center back seat
   D. next to the driver

2. According to this article, drivers should ___.
   A. use headlights when it's foggy
   B. always drive sixty miles per hour
   C. ride in safety seats
   D. make mistakes

3. According to this article, drivers should NOT ___.
   A. be prepared for other drivers' mistakes
   B. look before changing lanes
   C. use their windshield wipers in the rain
   D. use a cell phone while they're driving

4. A driver who *tailgates* ___.
   A. is a slow driver
   B. drives too close to the car ahead
   C. stops without warning
   D. is a careful driver

5. We can infer that *the windshield* in paragraph 3 ___.
   A. stops the car
   B. cleans the car
   C. is in the back of the car
   D. is in the front of the car

6. *May cause drowsiness* means the medicine ___.
   A. is old
   B. is bad for you
   C. might make you tired
   D. might make you nervous

Narrative reading passages offer practice with simple newspaper and magazine articles on topics such as safe driving practices, cross-cultural expectations, the education system, and nutrition. Reading tips highlight key concepts and skills such as differentiating facts and inferences and recognizing signal words.

Reading comprehension exercises in multiple-choice formats help students prepare for the reading section of standardized tests.

Check-up tests allow a quick assessment of student achievement and help prepare students for the kinds of test items found on standardized tests.

More complete **Achievement Tests** for each unit, including listening test items, are available as reproducible masters and printable disk files in the Teacher's Guide with Multilevel Activity & Achievement Test Book and CD-ROM. They are also available in the companion Activity & Test Prep Workbook.

Vocabulary checklists and **language skill checklists** help students review words they have learned, keep track of the skills they are developing, and identify vocabulary and skills they need to continue to work on. These lists promote student persistence as students assess their own skills and check off all the ways they are succeeding as language learners.

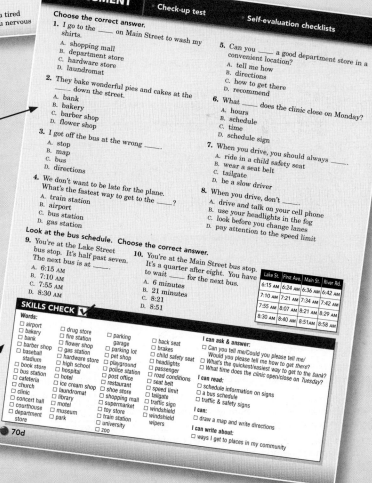

ASSESSMENT · Check-up test · Self-evaluation checklists

Choose the correct answer.

1. I go to the ___ on Main Street to wash my shirts.
   A. shopping mall
   B. department store
   C. hardware store
   D. laundromat

2. They bake wonderful pies and cakes at the ___ down the street.
   A. bank
   B. bakery
   C. barber shop
   D. flower shop

3. I got off the bus at the wrong ___.
   A. stop
   B. map
   C. bus
   D. directions

4. We don't want to be late for the plane. What's the fastest way to get to the ___?
   A. train station
   B. airport
   C. bus station
   D. gas station

5. Can you ___ a good department store in a convenient location?
   A. tell me how
   B. directions
   C. how to get there
   D. recommend

6. What ___ does the clinic close on Monday?
   A. hours
   B. schedule
   C. time
   D. schedule sign

7. When you drive, you should always ___.
   A. ride in a child safety seat
   B. wear a seat belt
   C. tailgate
   D. be a slow driver

8. When you drive, don't ___.
   A. drive and talk on your cell phone
   B. use your headlights in the fog
   C. look before you change lanes
   D. pay attention to the speed limit

Look at the bus schedule. Choose the correct answer.

9. You're at the Lake Street bus stop. It's half past seven. The next bus is at ___.
   A. 6:15 AM
   B. 7:10 AM
   C. 7:55 AM
   D. 8:30 AM

10. You're at the Main Street bus stop. It's a quarter after eight. You have to wait ___ for the next bus.
    A. 6 minutes
    B. 21 minutes
    C. 8:21
    D. 8:51

Lake St.	First Ave.	Main St.	River Rd.
6:15 AM	6:24 AM	6:36 AM	6:42 AM
7:10 AM	7:21 AM	7:34 AM	7:42 AM
7:55 AM	8:07 AM	8:21 AM	8:29 AM
8:30 AM	8:40 AM	8:51AM	8:58 AM

SKILLS CHECK ✓

Words:

☐ airport	☐ drug store	☐ parking garage	☐ back seat
☐ bakery	☐ fire station	☐ parking lot	☐ brakes
☐ bank	☐ flower shop	☐ pet shop	☐ child safety seat
☐ barber shop	☐ gas station	☐ playground	☐ headlights
☐ baseball stadium	☐ hardware store	☐ police station	☐ passenger
☐ book store	☐ high school	☐ post office	☐ road conditions
☐ bus station	☐ hospital	☐ restaurant	☐ seat belt
☐ cafeteria	☐ hotel	☐ shoe store	☐ speed limit
☐ church	☐ ice cream shop	☐ shopping mall	☐ tailgate
☐ clinic	☐ laundromat	☐ supermarket	☐ traffic sign
☐ concert hall	☐ library	☐ toy store	☐ windshield
☐ courthouse	☐ motel	☐ train station	☐ windshield wipers
☐ department store	☐ museum	☐ university	
	☐ park	☐ zoo	

I can ask & answer:
☐ Can you tell me/Could you please tell me/ Would you please tell me how to get *there*?
☐ What's the quickest/easiest way to get to the *bank*?
☐ What time does the *clinic* open/close on Tuesday?

I can read:
☐ schedule information on signs
☐ a bus schedule
☐ traffic & safety signs

I can:
☐ draw a map and write directions

I can write about:
☐ ways I get to places in my community

70d

Scope and Sequence

Unit	Topics, Vocabulary, & Math	Grammar	Functional Communication	Listening & Pronunciation	Writing
1	• Describing present, past, & future actions • Birthdays & gifts • Telling about friendships • Days of the week • Months of the year • Seasons • The calendar & dates • Reading a date using ordinal numbers • School registration • The American education system	• Tense review: Simple Present, Present Continuous, Simple Past, Future: Going to • Like to • Time expressions • Indirect object pronouns	• Talking about likes & dislikes • Describing future plans & intentions	• Listening for correct tense in information questions • Pronouncing contrastive stress	• Writing about your last birthday • Writing about a friendship • Filling out a personal information form • Filling out a school registration form
2	• Food • Buying food • Being a guest at mealtime • Describing food preferences • School personnel & locations • Reading a school floor plan • Reading skill: Facts & inferences • Following written instructions • Technology: Setting up a computer	• Count/Non-count nouns	• Asking the location of items • Making a suggestion • Complimenting about food	• Listening for key words to determine subject matter of conversations • Pronouncing reduced *for*	• Making a list of foods in the kitchen and their location • Writing about favorite foods • Writing about school • Writing information in a chart
3	• Buying food • Describing food • Eating in a restaurant • Recipes • Units of measure & abbreviations • Supermarket sections • Reading a store directory • Supermarket receipts • Food labels • Restaurant menus • Dollar amounts in numerals	• Partitives • Count/Non-count nouns • Imperatives	• Asking for information • Asking for and making recommendations about food • Giving and following instructions	• Listening for key words to determine subject matter of conversations • Pronouncing of before consonants & vowels	• Making a shopping list • Writing a recipe • Writing about a special meal • Writing about a supermarket
Gazette	• Food shopping • Ordering fast food • Interpreting statistics about food • Culture concept: Where people shop for food around the world	• Simple past tense • Present tense • Count/Non-count nouns	• Describing people's customs & consumer behavior	• Listening to & interpreting announcements in a supermarket correctly	• Writing an e-mail or instant message to tell about the meals you eat
4	• Telling about the future • Identifying life events • Health problems & injuries • Probability • Possibility • Talking about favorite season • Warnings • Calling in sick • Calling school to report absence • Cross-cultural expectations • Reading skill: Signal words	• Future tense: Will • Time expressions • Might	• Asking & telling about future events • Asking for and making predictions • Asking for repetition • Expressing fears • Providing reassurance • Social interaction: Offers & invitations	• Listening to & responding appropriately to a speaker in a telephone conversation • Pronouncing *going to*	• Writing a note to a child's teacher to explain an absence • Writing about your future • Writing about plans for the weekend • Writing invitations

CORRELATION and PLACEMENT KEY

Side by Side Plus 2 correlates with these standards-based curriculum levels and assessment system score ranges.

For correlation keys to other major state and local curriculum frameworks, please visit:
www.pearsonlongman.com/sidebysideplus

NRS (National Reporting System) Educational Functioning Level	High Beginning
SPL (Student Performance Level)	3
CASAS (Comprehensive Adult Student Assessment System)	191–200
BEST Plus (Basic English Skills Test)	418–438
BEST Oral Interview	29–41
BEST Literacy	36–46

Life Skills, Civics, & Test Preparation	EFF	SCANS/Employment Competencies	CASAS	LAUSD	Florida*
• Asking & answering personal information questions • Providing information about family members • Calendars, dates, & ordinal numbers • Writing months, days, & dates • Writing ordinal numbers • Registering for school • Reading a community center activity calendar • Identifying types of schools • The American education system	• Interact in a way that is friendly • Identify family relationships • Identify supportive friendships • Work together	• Sociability • Allocate time • Participate as a member of a team • Understand an organizational system (the education system)	0.1.2, 0.1.6, 0.2.1, 0.2.2, 0.2.4, 2.3.2, 2.5.5	1, 2, 3, 4, 5, 6, 7a, 11e, 13, 25	3.05.01, 3.08.03, 3.08.04, 3.14.01, 3.14.02, 3.14.04, 3.16.02
• School personnel & locations • Classroom instructions • School registration • Reading a class schedule • The education system • Learning skills: Chronological order, Steps in a process • Reading a diagram • Technology: Setting up a computer	• Manage resources: Identify those resources you have; Determine where they are • Understand, interpret, and work with symbolic information • Use technology	• Identify resources • See things in the mind's eye (Interpret a diagram) • Understand an organizational system (a school; the education system) • Work with technology	0.1.2, 0.1.4, 0.1.5, 2.5.5, 4.5.1, 4.5.2	9a, 10c, 12, 13, 14, 15, 59, 60, 61	3.04.01, 3.07.05, 3.14.02, 3.14.03, 3.16.06
• Food containers & quantities • Food weights & measures: Abbreviations • Asking about availability & location of items in a store • Food advertisements • Food packaging & label information • Reading a supermarket receipt • Reading a menu & computing costs • Ordering a meal • Learning skill: Categorizing food	• Manage resources • Understand, interpret, & work with numbers • Work together • Gather, analyze, & use information	• Identify resources • Allocate money • Serve clients/customers • Participate as a member of a team • Acquire & evaluate information	0.1.2, 0.1.3, 1.1.4, 1.1.7, 1.2.1, 1.2.2, 1.3.8, 1.3.9, 1.6.1, 2.6.4, 3.5.1, 6.6.4, 8.1.4	27, 30, 31, 32, 34, 35, 36	3.07.05, 3.08.05, 3.11.01, 3.11.03, 3.12.03, 3.16.06
• Interpreting a reading about customs & consumer behavior • Interpreting statistical facts • Ordering fast food • Interpreting store announcements	• Analyze information • Identify community needs & resources • Respect others & value diversity	• Acquire & evaluate information • Identify resources • Work with cultural diversity	0.1.2, 1.1.7, 1.3.8	34, 36	3.07.05, 3.15.12, 3.16.02, 3.16.06
• Small talk at work & at school • Invitations & offers • Asking for clarification • Interpreting a narrative reading about cross-cultural expectations	• Interact in a way that is friendly • Seek input from others • Identify problems • Provide for family members' needs • Create a vision & goals for the future • Respect others & value diversity	• Sociability • Identify goal-relevant activities • Identify workplace safety problems & state warnings • Self-management • Responsibility • Work with cultural diversity	0.1.2, 0.1.4, 0.1.6, 0.2.4, 2.5.5, 4.4.1	7, 9, 11, 16a, 55a	3.02.01, 3.02.02, 3.02.03, 3.03.02, 3.05.02, 3.05.03, 3.05.04, 3.07.03, 3.15.12, 3.16.02

EFF: Equipped for the Future (Content standards, Common activities, & Key activities for Citizen/Community Member, Worker, & Parent/Family role maps; EFF Communication and Reflection/Evaluation skills are covered in every unit)

SCANS: Secretary's Commission on Achieving Necessary Skills (U.S. Department of Labor)

CASAS: Comprehensive Adult Student Assessment System

LAUSD: Los Angeles Unified School District (ESL Beginning High content standards)

Florida: Adult ESOL High Beginning Standardized Syllabi

(*Florida benchmarks 3.15.01, 3.15.02, 3.15,03, 3.15.04, 3.15.05, 3.15.11, 3.15.13, 3.16.01, 3.16.02, 3.16.05, 3.16.06, 3.16.07, 3.16.09, 3.17.01, 3.17.02, and 3.17.03 are covered in every unit.)

Scope and Sequence

Unit	Topics, Vocabulary, & Math	Grammar	Functional Communication	Listening & Pronunciation	Writing
5	• Making comparisons • Advice • Expressing opinions • Agreement & disagreement • Teenager & parent relationships • Community features & problems • Shopping • Advertisements • Reading skill: Inference questions • Civics: Letters to the editor	• Comparatives • Should • Possessive pronouns	• Asking for & giving advice • Agreeing & disagreeing • Comparing things, places, & people • Exchanging opinions • Compliments	• Listening to determine the subject matter of a conversation • Pronouncing yes/no questions with *or*	• Writing about a comparison of two places • Writing a letter to the editor of a newspaper
6	• Describing people, places, & things • Shopping in a department store • Expressing opinions • Store directories • Returning & exchanging items • Using an ATM • Checks • Store return policies • Identifying different types of stores and comparing prices, quality of products, convenience, & service	• Superlatives	• Expressing an opinion • Offering assistance	• Listening to determine a speaker's attitude or opinion • Pronouncing linking words with duplicated consonants	• Writing about the most important person in your life • Writing checks to pay bills
Gazette	• Interpreting numerical and descriptive facts about world records and geographic features • Culture concept: Recreation & entertainment around the world	• Superlatives • Adjectives with negative prefixes	• Interpreting factual statements • Describing	• Listening to and interpreting radio advertisements correctly	• Writing an e-mail or instant message to tell about a favorite vacation place

Life Skills, Civics, & Test Preparation	EFF	SCANS/Employment Competencies	CASAS	LAUSD	Florida*
• Small talk at work & at school • Thank-you notes • Expressing opinions • Teenager & parent relationships • Community features & problems • Comparing store products • Interpreting advertisements • Letters to the editor	• Seek input from others • Guide & support others • Identify supportive family relationships • Meet family needs & responsibilities • Advocate & influence • Gather, analyze, & use information • Work together	• Sociability • Decision making • Understand a social system (community) • Acquire & evaluate information • Participate as a member of a team	0.1.2, 0.1.4, 0.2.4, 1.2.1, 1.2.2	7, 10, 32	3.02.03, 3.03.02, 3.05.01, 3.05.02, 3.05.03, 3.05.04, 3.11.03, 3.14.01, 3.16.03
• Expressing pride in a child's personal qualities • Shopping requests & locating items • Comparing store prices, products, convenience, & service • Learning skills: Steps in a process; Categorizing types of products • Understanding ATM instructions • Interpreting a check • Problems with purchases • Returning & exchanging items • Store sales	• Interact in a way that is friendly • Identify a strong sense of family • Advocate & influence • Identify community resources • Use technology to accomplish goals • Work together • Gather, analyze, & use information • Use technology	• Sociability • Integrity/Honesty • Serve clients/customers • Identify resources • Participate as a member of a team • Acquire & evaluate information • Work with technology	0.1.3, 0.1.4, 1.3.3, 1.3.9, 1.6.3, 1.8.1, 1.8.2, 8.1.4	10a, 28, 29, 30, 33, 59	3.08.05, 3.08.06, 3.11.02, 3.11.03, 3.16.03
• Interpreting statistical facts • Interpreting radio advertisements	• Analyze & use information • Understand, interpret, & work with numbers • Respect others & value diversity	• Acquire & evaluate information • Work with cultural diversity	0.1.3, 1.3.9	30	3.15.12, 3.16.03

1

Review of Tenses:
Simple Present
Present Continuous
Simple Past
Future: Going to

Like to
Time Expressions
Indirect Object
Pronouns

- **Describing Present, Past, and Future Actions**
- **Birthdays and Gifts**
- **Telling About Friendships**

- **School Registration**
- **The Calendar and Dates**
- **Filling Out a Registration Form**
- **The American Education System**

VOCABULARY PREVIEW

Spring   *Summer*

Fall   *Winter*

1. Days of the Week
Sunday
Monday
Tuesday
Wednesday
Thursday
Friday
Saturday

2. Months of the Year
January   July
February   August
March   September
April   October
May   November
June   December

3. Seasons
spring
summer
fall / autumn
winter

What Do You Like to Do on the Weekend?

I We You They	like to
He She It	likes to

eat.

A. What do you like to do on the weekend?

B. I like to read.

A. What does Ron like to do on the weekend?

B. He likes to go to the mall.

1. *Mr. and Mrs. Johnson?*
watch TV

2. *Tom?*
play basketball

3. *Sally?*
go to the beach

4. *you and your friends?*
chat online

5. *your grandmother?*
go hiking

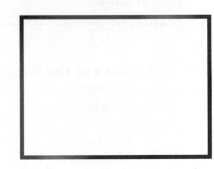

6. *you?*

cook	play	swim	write
cooks	plays	swims	writes
cooked	played	swam	wrote
cooking	playing	swimming	writing

Robert likes to cook.
He cooks every day.
He cooked yesterday.
He's cooking right now.
He's going to cook tomorrow.
As you can see, Robert REALLY likes to cook.

Irene likes to play the piano.
She plays the piano every day.
She played the piano yesterday.
She's playing the piano right now.
She's going to play the piano tomorrow.
As you can see, Irene REALLY likes to play
    the piano.

Jimmy and Patty like to swim.*
They swim every day.
They swam yesterday.
They're swimming right now.
They're going to swim tomorrow.
As you can see, Jimmy and Patty REALLY
    like to swim.

Jonathan likes to write.
He writes every day.
He wrote yesterday.
He's writing right now.
He's going to write tomorrow.
As you can see, Jonathan REALLY likes to
    write.

Using these questions, talk about the people above with students in your class.

What does _____ like to do?
What does he/she do every day?
What did he/she do yesterday?
What's he/she doing right now?
What's he/she going to do tomorrow?

What do _____ like to do?
What do they do every day?
What did they do yesterday?
What are they doing right now?
What are they going to do tomorrow?

Then use these questions to talk about other people you know.

* swim – swam

Are You Going to Cook Spaghetti This Week?

A. Are you going to cook spaghetti this week?

B. No, I'm not. I cooked spaghetti LAST week, and I don't like to cook spaghetti very often.

1. Are you going to watch videos today?

2. Are you going to drive downtown this weekend?

3. Is Mrs. Miller going to plant flowers this spring?

4. Is your father going to make pancakes this morning?

5. Are Mr. and Mrs. Jenkins going to the mall* this Saturday?

6. Are you and your friends going skiing this December?

7. Are you going to write letters tonight?

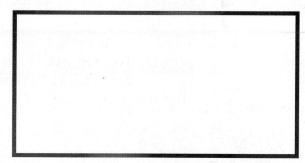

8. Is Dave going to clean his room this week?

9. Are you and your family going to WonderWorld this year?

10.

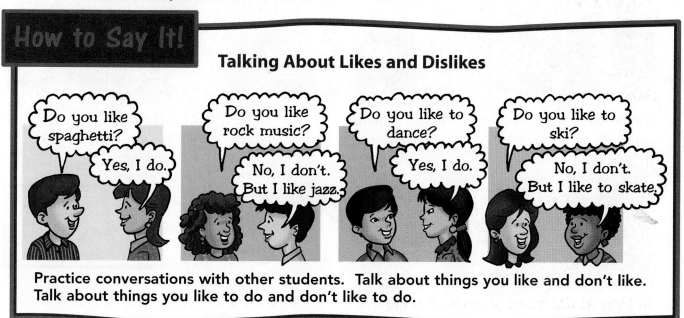

How to Say It!

Talking About Likes and Dislikes

Do you like spaghetti?

Yes, I do.

Do you like rock music?

No, I don't. But I like jazz.

Do you like to dance?

Yes, I do.

Do you like to ski?

No, I don't. But I like to skate.

Practice conversations with other students. Talk about things you like and don't like. Talk about things you like to do and don't like to do.

* going to the mall = going to go to the mall

What Are You Going to Give Your Wife?

| I'm going to give { my husband / my wife } a present. | I'm going to give { him / her } a present. |

A. What are you going to give your wife for her birthday?

B. I don't know. I can't give her a necklace. I gave her a necklace last year.

A. How about flowers?

B. No. I can't give her flowers. I gave her flowers two years ago.

A. Well, what are you going to give her?

B. I don't know. I really have to think about it.

A. What are you going to give your _____ for (his/her) birthday?

B. I don't know. I can't _____. I _____ last year.

A. How about _____?

B. No. I can't _____. I _____ two years ago.

A. Well, what are you going to give (him/her)?

B. I don't know. I really have to think about it.

1. *husband*
   a watch
   a briefcase

2. *girlfriend*
   perfume
   a bracelet

3. *boyfriend*
   a jacket
   a sweater

4. *grandmother*
   flowers
   candy

5. *daughter*
   a bicycle
   a doll

6.

What Did Your Parents Give You?

I	me
he	him
she	her
we	us
you	you
they	them

A. What did your parents give you for your birthday?

B. They gave me a CD player.

1. What did you give your parents for their anniversary?

a painting

2. What did Mr. Lee's grandchildren give him for his birthday?

a computer

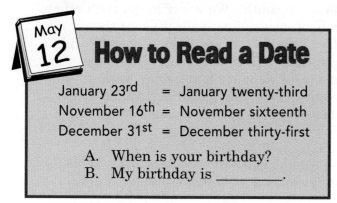

3. What did your children give you and your wife for your anniversary?

a plant

4. I forget. What did you give me for my last birthday?

a purple blouse with pink polka dots

MAY 12

How to Read a Date

January 23rd = January twenty-third
November 16th = November sixteenth
December 31st = December thirty-first

A. When is your birthday?
B. My birthday is _____.

SIDE by SIDE JOURNAL

Write in your journal about your last birthday. What did you do on your birthday? Did your family or friends give you any presents? Write about it.

VERY GOOD FRIENDS: EAST AND WEST

Eric and Susan are very good friends. They grew up together, they went to high school together, and they went to college together. Now Eric lives in California, and Susan lives in New Jersey. Even though they live far apart, they're still very good friends.

They write to each other very often. He writes her letters about life on the West Coast, and she writes him letters about life on the East Coast. They never forget each other's birthday. Last year he sent* her some CDs, and she sent him a wallet. Eric and Susan help each other very often. Last year he lent* her money when she was in the hospital, and she gave him advice when he lost* his job.

Eric and Susan like each other very much. They were always very good friends, and they still are.

VERY GOOD FRIENDS: NORTH AND SOUTH

Carlos and Maria are our very good friends. For many years we went to church together, we took vacations together, and our children played together. Now Carlos and Maria live in Florida, and we still live here in Wisconsin. Even though we live far apart, we're still very good friends.

We communicate with each other very often on the Internet. We send them messages about life up north, and they send us messages about life down south. We never forget each others' anniversaries. Last year we sent them Wisconsin cheese, and they sent us Florida oranges. We also help each other very often. Last year we lent them money when they bought a new van, and they gave us advice when we sold* our house and moved into a condominium.

We like each other very much. We were always very good friends, and we still are.

* send – sent   lose – lost
   lend – lent   sell – sold

8

✓ READING *CHECK-UP*

TRUE OR FALSE?

1. Eric and Susan are in high school.
2. Eric lives on the West Coast.
3. Susan sent Eric some CDs last year.
4. Susan was sick last year.
5. They were friends when they were children.
6. Carlos and Maria don't live in Wisconsin now.
7. Florida is in the north.
8. Carlos and Maria send messages on the Internet.
9. Carlos and Maria moved into a condominium last year.

LISTENING

Listen and choose the correct answer.

1. a. I like to play tennis.
   b. I'm going to play tennis.
2. a. I went to the beach.
   b. I go to the beach.
3. a. Yesterday morning.
   b. Tomorrow afternoon.
4. a. I gave them a plant.
   b. I'm going to give them a plant.
5. a. We went to the mall.
   b. We're going to the mall.
6. a. They sent messages last week.
   b. They send messages every week.
7. a. He gave her flowers.
   b. She gave him flowers.
8. a. Last weekend.
   b. Tomorrow morning.

IN YOUR OWN WORDS

FOR WRITING AND DISCUSSION

A VERY GOOD FRIEND

Do you have a very good friend who lives far away? Tell about your friendship.

How do you know each other?
How do you communicate with each other?
   (Do you call? write? send e-mail messages?)
What do you talk about or write about?
Do you send each other presents?
Do you help each other? How?

PRONUNCIATION *Contrastive Stress*

Listen. Then say it.

I'm not going to clean my room this week.
I cleaned my room LÁST week.

I'm not going to make pancakes this morning.
I made pancakes YÉSTERDAY morning.

Say it. Then listen.

I'm not going to watch videos tonight.
I watched videos LÁST night.

I'm not going to write letters this evening.
I wrote letters YÉSTERDAY evening.

GRAMMAR FOCUS

SIMPLE PRESENT TENSE

I We You They	cook.
He She It	cooks.

LIKE TO

I We You They	like to / don't like to	
He She It	likes to / doesn't like to	cook.

PRESENT CONTINUOUS TENSE

(I am)	I'm	
(He is) (She is) (It is)	He's She's It's	cooking.
(We are) (You are) (They are)	We're You're They're	

SIMPLE PAST TENSE

I He She It We You They	cooked.

FUTURE: GOING TO

I'm He's She's It's We're You're They're	going to cook.

Am	I	
Is	he she it	going to cook?
Are	we you they	

Yes,	I	am.
	he she it	is.
	we you they	are.

No,	I'm	not.
	he she it	isn't.
	we you they	aren't.

INDIRECT OBJECT PRONOUNS

He gave	me him her it us you them	a present.

PAST TIME EXPRESSIONS

yesterday
yesterday morning / afternoon / evening
last night
last week / weekend / month / year
last Sunday / Monday /. . ./ Saturday
last January / February /. . ./ December
last spring / summer / fall (autumn) / winter

IRREGULAR VERBS

drive – drove
give – gave
go – went
lend – lent
lose – lost
sell – sold
send – sent
swim – swam
write – wrote

Complete each sentence with the correct form of the verb.

drive	give	go	watch	write

1. My parents are _____ TV in the living room. They _____ TV every evening.
2. I _____ my car downtown yesterday. I don't like to _____ downtown very often.
3. Monica likes to _____ letters. Last night she _____ a letter to her grandfather.
4. I'm not going to _____ my brother a tie for his birthday. I _____ him a tie last year.
5. My wife and I _____ swimming very often. We _____ swimming last weekend.

Match the questions and answers.

_____ 6. What did your brother give you for your birthday?
_____ 7. What did you give your brother for his birthday?
_____ 8. What did your grandmother give your sister?
_____ 9. What did your grandfather give your brother?
_____ 10. What did you give your parents?
_____ 11. What did your parents give you for your birthday?

a. She gave her a necklace.
b. They gave me a CD player.
c. I gave them a painting.
d. He gave me a watch.
e. He gave him a shirt.
f. I gave him a briefcase.

10

1 CONVERSATION   GIVING PERSONAL INFORMATION

Look at the form. Practice the conversation with a classmate.

School Registration Form

NAME   Abdi   Hassan
     First   Last

ADDRESS 257 2nd Avenue   12B
      Number Street   Apartment

    New York   NY   10003
    City   State Zip Code

AGE   6   DATE OF BIRTH   10   06   01
                        Month Day Year

*We write:
October 6, 2001
10/06/01
| 1 0 | 0 6 | 0 1 |
Month   Day   Year

We say:
October sixth,
two thousand one

A. May I help you?

B. Yes, please. I want to register
my son for school.

A. Okay. What's his last name?

B. _____.

A. And his first name?

B. _____.

A. How old is he?

B. _____.

A. What's his date of birth?

B. _____.*

A. And what's your address?

B. _____.

2 TEAMWORK   REGISTERING FOR SCHOOL

Work with a classmate. This parent is registering her daughter for school.
Fill out the form and practice the conversation. (Use any information you wish.)

School Registration Form

NAME   _____   _____
     First   Last

ADDRESS _____
      Number Street   Apartment

    _____
    City   State Zip Code

AGE _____   DATE OF BIRTH ____ ____ ____
                      Month Day Year

A. May I help you?

B. Yes, please. I want to register
my daughter for school.

A. Okay. What's her last name?

B. _____.

A. And her first name?

B. _____.

A. How old is she?

B. _____.

A. What's her date of birth?

B. _____.

A. And what's your address?

B. _____.

Read about the activities at the Canton Community Center. When are they?
Circle the dates on the calendar below.

		JANUARY				
S	M	T	W	Th	F	S
		1	2	3	4
(5)	6	7	8	9	10	11
12	13	14	15	16	17	18
19	20	21	22	23	24	25
26	27	28	29	30	31	

		FEBRUARY				
S	M	T	W	Th	F	S
						1
(2)	3	4	5	6	7	8
9	10	11	12	13	14	15
16	17	18	19	20	21	22
23	24	25	26	27	28	

		MARCH				
S	M	T	W	Th	F	S
						1
(2)	3	4	5	6	7	8
9	10	11	12	13	14	15
16	17	18	19	20	21	22
23	24	25	26	27	28	29
30	31					

		APRIL				
S	M	T	W	Th	F	S
		1	2	3	4	5
(6)	7	8	9	10	11	12
13	14	15	16	17	18	19
20	21	22	23	24	25	26
27	28	29	30			

		MAY				
S	M	T	W	Th	F	S
				1	2	3
(4)	5	6	7	8	9	10
11	12	13	14	15	16	17
18	19	20	21	22	23	24
25	26	27	28	29	30	31

		JUNE				
S	M	T	W	Th	F	S
1	2	3	4	5	6	7
(8)	9	10	11	12	13	14
15	16	17	18	19	20	21
22	23	24	25	26	27	28
29	30					

Activities at Your Community Center – January to June

1. There are movies on the first Sunday of every month.

2. The Center is celebrating Martin Luther King, Jr. Day on the third Monday in January.

3. There are jazz concerts on the second Friday of every month.

4. There's a pancake breakfast on April twentieth.

5. Arnold McCall is reading from his new book, *When I Was Young*, on May thirtieth.

6. There's a dance for young people on February twenty-second.

7. There are swimming classes every Thursday in June.

8. Marta Fernandez is giving a piano concert on April thirteenth.

9. There's a rock concert on January twenty-fifth.

10. High school students can get help with their homework on the fourth Tuesday of every month.

11. You can go hiking in the White Mountains on May eighteenth and June fifteenth.

12. Chef Marconi is giving cooking classes on the second and fourth Wednesdays in June.

13. There's a ski trip to Mount Snow on January twenty-first.

14. Boys and girls can play basketball on the first and third Saturday of every month.

15. You can go skating every Wednesday from February fifth to March nineteenth.

16. There's a trip to Sandy Beach on June twenty-eighth.

17. There are exercise classes every Thursday from April twenty-fourth to May twenty-ninth.

Read the article and answer the questions.

The American Education System

There are many different kinds of schools in the United States. Most children go to public schools that are free, but there are also private schools that students pay to attend. Free public education begins with kindergarten (the first year of elementary school) and finishes with the twelfth grade (the last year of high school).

Many parents send their young children to day-care centers and pre-schools before kindergarten. They pay for their children to attend these schools. In most states, children do not have to attend kindergarten, but they must start elementary school in the first grade when they're six years old. They have to attend school for ten years or more. Each state has its own law about when students can leave school.

Most elementary schools have five grades plus kindergarten. After elementary school, children usually go to middle school for sixth, seventh, and eighth grade. Most students enter high school in the ninth grade and graduate after four years.

Many people continue their education after high school at a technical or vocational school, a two-year community college, a four-year college, or a university. Technical and vocational schools teach

students the skills they need for a job. Community colleges also have vocational programs that prepare students for work.

Four-year colleges can be very expensive. Many students spend their first two years of college at a community college. After that, they can apply to study for two more years at a four-year college and then graduate. Some colleges are part of large universities. These universities also have graduate schools where students continue to study after they graduate from college. Students who want to be doctors, for example, go to college for four years and then study at a medical school in a university.

1. Kindergarten is the first year of _____.
   A. pre-school
   B. day care
   C. elementary school
   D. middle school

2. Students usually go to middle school for _____.
   A. four years
   B. three years
   C. two years
   D. one year

3. Students have to pay to go to _____.
   A. kindergarten
   B. high school
   C. middle school
   D. private school

4. Children usually have to go to school when they're _____.
   A. three years old
   B. four years old
   C. five years old
   D. six years old

5. The tenth grade is usually the _____ year of high school.
   A. second
   B. third
   C. first
   D. fourth

6. A medical school is part of a _____.
   A. community college
   B. four-year college
   C. university
   D. vocational school

Choose the correct answer.

1. Brian is very athletic. Every weekend he likes to _____.
   A. chat online
   B. go hiking
   C. watch videos
   D. cook

2. My brother likes clothes. I'm going to give him a _____ for his birthday.
   A. briefcase
   B. CD player
   C. sweater
   D. plant

3. My parents _____ their house and bought a condominium.
   A. sent
   B. gave
   C. moved
   D. sold

4. I like to listen to music on my _____.
   A. CD player
   B. wallet
   C. watch
   D. painting

5. Every day I _____ with my friends over the Internet.
   A. call
   B. grow up
   C. send
   D. communicate

6. When I have a problem, my parents always give me good _____.
   A. advice
   B. message
   C. friends
   D. letters

7. I live on the West Coast, and you live on the East Coast. We live _____ each other.
   A. near
   B. far apart from
   C. between
   D. next to

8. I want to _____ my children for school.
   A. registration
   B. form
   C. registration form
   D. register

9. My seven-year-old daughter goes to a very good _____.
   A. middle school
   B. vocational school
   C. elementary school
   D. high school

10. My birthday is _____.
    A. the first Thursday of every month
    B. November 16th
    C. April 10, 1991
    D. from May ninth to May twelfth

SKILLS CHECK ✓

Words:
☐ chat online
☐ clean
☐ cook
☐ drive
☐ go *hiking*
☐ go to *the mall*
☐ make *pancakes*
☐ plant
☐ play *basketball*
☐ play the *piano*
☐ read
☐ swim
☐ watch TV
☐ write

Days of the week:
☐ Sunday
☐ Monday
☐ Tuesday
☐ Wednesday
☐ Thursday
☐ Friday
☐ Saturday

Months of the year:
☐ January
☐ February
☐ March
☐ April
☐ May
☐ June
☐ July
☐ August
☐ September
☐ October
☐ November
☐ December

Types of schools:
☐ day-care center
☐ pre-school
☐ elementary school
☐ middle school
☐ high school
☐ technical school
☐ vocational school
☐ community college
☐ college
☐ university
☐ graduate school
☐ medical school

I can ask & answer:
☐ What do you do every day?
☐ What are you doing right now?
☐ What are you going to do tomorrow?
☐ What did you do yesterday?
☐ What do you like to do?
☐ Do you like *rock music*?
☐ Do you like to *ski*?

I can:
☐ read dates & use a calendar
☐ fill out a registration form

I can write about:
☐ my last birthday
☐ a close friendship

2

Count/Non-Count Nouns

- Food
- Buying Food
- Being a Guest at Mealtime
- Describing Food Preferences
- School Personnel and Locations

- Reading a School Floor Plan
- Reading Skill: Fact and Inference Questions
- Following Written Instructions
- Technology: Setting Up a Computer

VOCABULARY PREVIEW

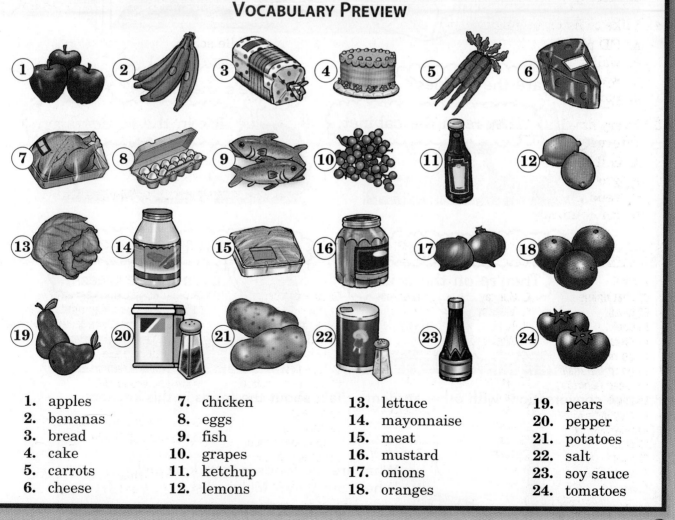

1. apples	7. chicken	13. lettuce	19. pears
2. bananas	8. eggs	14. mayonnaise	20. pepper
3. bread	9. fish	15. meat	21. potatoes
4. cake	10. grapes	16. mustard	22. salt
5. carrots	11. ketchup	17. onions	23. soy sauce
6. cheese	12. lemons	18. oranges	24. tomatoes

Practice conversations with other students. Talk about the foods in this kitchen.

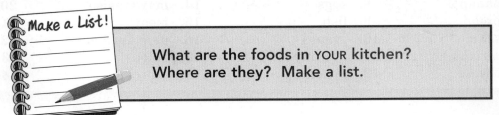

Make a List!

What are the foods in YOUR kitchen?
Where are they? Make a list.

12

Let's Make Sandwiches for Lunch!

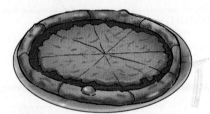

1. Let's make pizza for lunch!
   cheese

2. Let's make some fresh lemonade!
   lemons

3. Let's make a salad for dinner!
   lettuce

4. Let's make an omelet for breakfast!
   eggs

5. Let's bake a cake for dessert!
   flour

6. Let's make some fresh orange juice for breakfast!
   oranges

7. Let's have french fries with our hamburgers!
   potatoes

8. Let's have meatballs with our spaghetti!
   meat

9.

How Much Milk Do You Want?

how much?	how many?
too much	too many
a little	a few

A. How much milk do you want?

B. Not too much. Just a little.

A. Okay. Here you are.

B. Thanks.

A. How many cookies do you want?

B. Not too many. Just a few.

A. Okay. Here you are.

B. Thanks.

1. *rice*

2. *french fries*

3. *ice cream*

4. *coffee*

5. *meatballs*

6.

Some of your friends are having dinner at your home. How do they like the food? Ask them.

A. How do you like the _____?

B. I think (it's / they're) delicious.

A. I'm glad you like (it / them). Would you care for some more?

B. Yes, please. But not (too much / too many). Just (a little / a few).
My doctor says that (too much / too many) _____ (is / are) bad for my health.

chocolate cake

cookies

ice cream

How to Say It!

Complimenting About Food

A. This *chicken* is delicious!*
B. I'm glad you like it.

A. These *potatoes* are delicious!*
B. I'm glad you like them.

* delicious / very good / excellent / wonderful / fantastic

Practice conversations with other students.

15

TWO BAGS OF GROCERIES

Henry is at the supermarket, and he's really upset. He just bought some groceries, and he can't believe he just spent* sixty dollars! He bought only a few oranges, a few apples, a little milk, a little ice cream, and a few eggs.

He also bought just a little coffee, a few onions, a few bananas, a little rice, a little cheese, and a few lemons. He didn't buy very much fish, he didn't buy very many grapes, and he didn't buy very much meat.

Henry just spent sixty dollars, but he's walking out of the supermarket with only two bags of groceries. No wonder he's upset!

* spend – spent

✔ **READING** *CHECK-UP*

Q & A

Using these models, make questions and answers based on the story.

A. How many *oranges* did he buy?
B. He bought only a few *oranges*.

A. How much *milk* did he buy?
B. He bought only a little *milk*.

How About You?

What did YOU buy the last time you went to the supermarket?

I bought { a few . . .
{ a little . . .

Listen and choose what the people are talking about.

1. a. cake   b. carrots
2. a. fish   b. potatoes
3. a. cookies   b. milk
4. a. cheese   b. meatballs
5. a. eggs   b. butter
6. a. rice   b. french fries
7. a. oranges   b. salad
8. a. lemonade   b. lemons

DELICIOUS!

Lucy likes french fries. In fact, she eats them all the time. Her friends often tell her that she eats too many french fries, but Lucy doesn't think so. She thinks they're delicious.

Fred likes ice cream. In fact, he eats it all the time. His doctor often tells him that he eats too much ice cream, but Fred doesn't think so. He thinks it's delicious.

TASTES TERRIBLE!

Daniel doesn't like vegetables. In fact, he never eats them. His parents often tell him that vegetables are good for him, but Daniel doesn't care. He thinks they taste terrible.

Alice doesn't like yogurt. In fact, she never eats it. Her children often tell her that yogurt is good for her, but Alice doesn't care. She thinks it tastes terrible.

ON YOUR OWN

Tell about foods you like.

What foods do you think are delicious?
How often do you eat them?
Are they good for you, or are they bad for you?

Tell about foods you don't like.

What foods do you think taste terrible?
How often do you eat them?
Are they good for you, or are they bad for you?

17

PRONUNCIATION   Reduced *for*

Listen. Then say it.

Let's make a salad for dinner!

Let's make eggs for breakfast!

Would you care for some more cake?

It's bad for my health.

Say it. Then listen.

Let's make pizza for lunch!

Let's have ice cream for dessert!

Would you care for some more cookies?

They're bad for my health.

SIDE by SIDE JOURNAL

Write in your journal about your favorite foods.
What are they? How often do you eat them?
Why do you like them?

GRAMMAR FOCUS

COUNT / NON-COUNT NOUNS

There isn't any	bread. lettuce. flour.

There aren't any	apples. eggs. lemons.

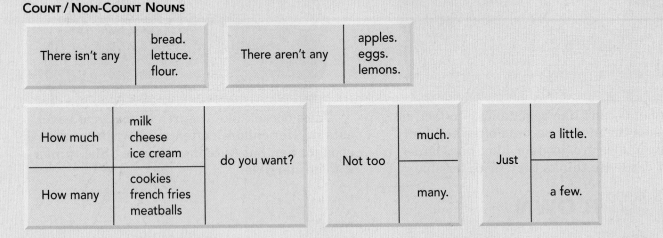

How much	milk cheese ice cream	do you want?
How many	cookies french fries meatballs	

Not too	much. many.

Just	a little. a few.

Choose the correct word.

1. We can't make a cake now.
   There (isn't   aren't) any flour.

2. There (isn't   aren't) any mayonnaise
   in the refrigerator.

3. We can't make an omelet.
   There (isn't   aren't) any eggs.

4. I don't want too (much   many) ice cream.
   Just a (little   few).

5. How (much   many) cake do you want?

6. I don't want too (much   many) cookies.
   Just a (little   few).

7. I bought just a (little   few) meat today.

8. My doctor often tells me that I eat too
   (much   many) desserts.

9. I bought a (little   few) carrots and a
   (little   few) cheese at the store.

10. How (much   many) rice did you buy?

11. I ate too (much   many) french fries!

1 CONVERSATION ASKING & GIVING LOCATION OF SCHOOL PERSONNEL

Practice conversations with a classmate.

A. Where's the _____?

B. He's/She's in the _____.

1. school nurse
   nurse's office

2. librarian
   library

3. guidance counselor
   guidance office

4. cafeteria worker
   cafeteria

5. security officer
   hall

6. school secretary
   school office

7. principal
   principal's office

8. music teacher
   auditorium

9. P.E. teacher
   gym

2 SCHOOL CONNECTIONS PEOPLE & LOCATIONS IN YOUR SCHOOL

Fill in the chart with information about some people who work in your school.

NAME	JOB	LOCATION AT SCHOOL

18a

Look at the floor plan of Madison Middle School and answer the questions.

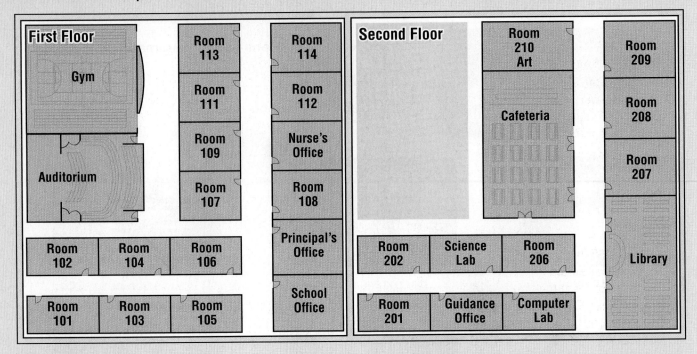

1. The school office is _____.
   A. next to Room 102
   B. across from the gym
   C. on the second floor
   D. next to the principal's office

2. There are _____ offices in Madison Middle School.
   A. two
   B. three
   C. four
   D. five

3. The nurse's office and _____ are on different floors.
   A. the library
   B. the principal's office
   C. Room 107
   D. the school office

4. Students go to the first floor when _____.
   A. it's time for lunch
   B. they feel sick
   C. they want to use a computer
   D. they're looking for books to read

5. Room 208 is probably noisy at noon because _____.
   A. it's next to the library
   B. it's on the second floor
   C. it's across from the cafeteria
   D. it's near the computer lab

6. The librarian and the _____ work on different floors.
   A. guidance counselor
   B. science teacher
   C. lunchroom monitor
   D. P.E. teacher

Reading Tip   Facts and Inferences

Fact questions ask for information you can find in a reading. Question 1 is a fact question. The floor plan shows you that the school office is next to the principal's office.

To answer **inference questions**, you have to think about information in a reading and put it together with other

things you know about the subject. Question 4 is an inference question. To answer it, you have to know what students do in different rooms of a school. That information is not on the floor plan.

What are the other inference questions on this page? What information do you need to know to answer them?

Read the instructions for setting up a new computer and answer the questions.

- Place the CPU and the monitor on a table or desk.
- There are several ports (openings) for cables on the back of your CPU. The port for the power cable is in the center, near the top. Connect the power cable to the port. Plug the other end of the power cable into an outlet with a surge protector.
- Connect the monitor cable to the port below the power cable port. Connect the other end of the cable to your monitor.
- There are three USB ports below the monitor port. Connect the cable on your keyboard to a USB port.
- Connect the mouse cable to a port on your keyboard.
- To use the Internet, you need an Ethernet cable and a modem. Connect the cable to an Ethernet port on the back of your CPU. There are two Ethernet ports at the bottom of the CPU below the USB ports. Connect the other end of the Ethernet cable to your modem.
- Turn on your computer and monitor. Use the power button on the front of your CPU.
- To finish setting up your computer, follow the instructions on the screen.
- To add a printer to your computer, connect the printer cable to a USB port on the back of your CPU. Then follow the instructions that come with your printer.

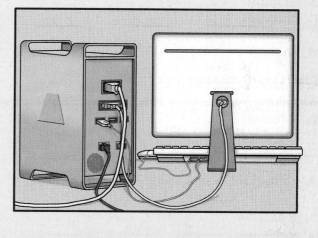

1. Plug your _____ into an outlet with a surge protector.
   A. mouse cable
   B. keyboard cable
   C. power cable
   D. Ethernet cable

2. The monitor port is on the back of the _____.
   A. keyboard
   B. CPU
   C. printer
   D. modem

3. There are three _____ on the back of the CPU.
   A. USB ports
   B. power cable ports
   C. Ethernet ports
   D. monitor ports

4. Connect the cable on your mouse to _____.
   A. a cable on your keyboard
   B. a port on your keyboard
   C. a port on your CPU
   D. an Ethernet cable

5. To use the Internet, you need _____.
   A. a printer
   B. a mouse
   C. a surge protector
   D. a modem and an Ethernet cable

6. You can use the same ports for the printer and the _____ cables.
   A. Ethernet
   B. monitor
   C. keyboard
   D. power

Choose the correct answer.

1. Do you want to bake some _____ today?
   A. salad
   B. ice cream
   C. cookies
   D. coffee

2. When I'm thirsty, I usually like to drink _____.
   A. lemons
   B. lettuce
   C. mayonnaise
   D. milk

3. Aunt Clara's _____ always tastes delicious.
   A. kitchen
   B. chicken
   C. cabinet
   D. counter

4. My favorite dessert is _____.
   A. cake
   B. ketchup
   C. mustard
   D. pepper

5. My daughter doesn't like yogurt. She thinks it tastes _____.
   A. excellent
   B. delicious
   C. terrible
   D. fantastic

6. Mr. and Mrs. Mendoza _____ seventy-five dollars at the supermarket.
   A. spent
   B. lent
   C. bought
   D. sold

7. The _____ is usually in our school's halls all day.
   A. P.E. teacher
   B. guidance counselor
   C. cafeteria worker
   D. security officer

8. The school secretary works in the _____.
   A. computer lab
   B. school office
   C. guidance office
   D. gym

9. When students at our school feel sick, they go to the _____.
   A. auditorium
   B. cafeteria
   C. nurse's office
   D. guidance office

10. There are three _____ on the back of the CPU.
    A. printers
    B. ports
    C. monitors
    D. keyboards

SKILLS CHECK ✓

Words:

☐ apple pie ☐ french fries ☐ onions ☐ spaghetti ☐ school nurse
☐ apples ☐ grapes ☐ orange juice ☐ sugar ☐ school secretary
☐ bananas ☐ hamburgers ☐ tea ☐ security officer
☐ bread ☐ ice cream ☐ oranges ☐ tomatoes
☐ butter ☐ ketchup ☐ pears ☐ vegetables ☐ auditorium
☐ cake ☐ lemonade ☐ pepper ☐ yogurt ☐ cafeteria
☐ carrots ☐ lemons ☐ pizza ☐ computer lab
☐ cheese ☐ lettuce ☐ potatoes ☐ cafeteria worker ☐ guidance office
☐ chicken ☐ mayonnaise ☐ rice ☐ guidance counselor ☐ gym
☐ coffee ☐ meat ☐ salad ☐ hall
☐ cookies ☐ meatballs ☐ salt ☐ librarian ☐ library
☐ eggs ☐ milk ☐ sandwich ☐ music teacher ☐ nurse's office
☐ fish ☐ mustard ☐ soda ☐ P.E. teacher ☐ principal's office
☐ flour ☐ omelet ☐ soy sauce ☐ principal ☐ school office

I can ask & answer:
☐ Where are the *cookies*?
☐ Where's the *cheese*?
☐ How much *milk* do you want?
☐ How many *cookies* do you want?

I can compliment about food:
☐ This *chicken* is/These *potatoes* are delicious!

I can write about:
☐ my favorite foods

I can:
☐ interpret a floor plan diagram
☐ follow instructions for setting up a computer

3

Partitives
Count/Non-Count Nouns
Imperatives

- Buying Food
- Describing Food
- Eating in a Restaurant
- Recipes
- Supermarket Sections

- Reading a Store Directory
- Supermarket Receipts
- Food Labels
- Restaurant Menus

VOCABULARY PREVIEW

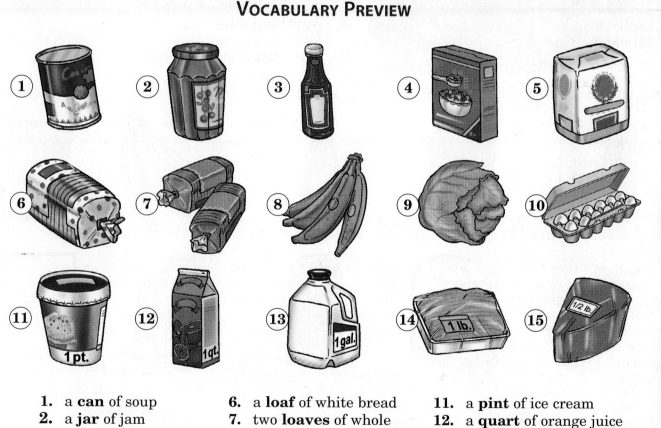

1. a **can** of soup
2. a **jar** of jam
3. a **bottle** of ketchup
4. a **box** of cereal
5. a **bag** of flour

6. a **loaf** of white bread
7. two **loaves** of whole wheat bread
8. a **bunch** of bananas
9. a **head** of lettuce
10. a **dozen** eggs

11. a **pint** of ice cream
12. a **quart** of orange juice
13. a **gallon** of milk
14. a **pound** of meat
15. a **half pound** } of cheese
    half a pound

19

Do We Need Anything from the Supermarket?

My Shopping List

a can of soup
a jar of jam
a bottle of ketchup
a box of cereal
a bag of flour
a loaf of white bread
2 loaves of whole wheat bread
a bunch of bananas
2 bunches of carrots

a head of lettuce
a dozen eggs

a pt.* of ice cream
a qt.* of orange juice
a gal.* of milk
a lb.* of meat
1/2 lb.* of cheese

* pt. = pint
qt. = quart
gal. = gallon
lb. = pound

A. Do we need anything from the supermarket?

B. Yes. We need a loaf of bread.

A. A loaf of bread?

B. Yes.

A. Anything else?

B. No. Just a loaf of bread.

1.   2.   3.   4.   5.

6.   7.   8.   9.   10.

Make a Shopping List!

What do you need from the supermarket?
Make a shopping list.

How Much Does a Head of Lettuce Cost?

1¢	$.01	one cent	$1.00	one dollar
25¢	$.25	twenty-five cents	$10.00	ten dollars

A. How much does **a head of lettuce** cost?

B. **A dollar ninety-five.*** ($1.95)

A. A DOLLAR NINETY-FIVE?! That's a lot of money!

B. You're right. **Lettuce** is very expensive this week.

* $1.95 = { a dollar ninety-five
one dollar and ninety-five cents

A. How much does **a pound of apples** cost?

B. **Two eighty-nine.*** ($2.89)

A. TWO EIGHTY-NINE?! That's a lot of money!

B. You're right. **Apples** are very expensive this week.

* $2.89 = { two eighty-nine
two dollars and eighty-nine cents

1.

2.

3.

4.

5.

6.

7.

8.

READING

NOTHING TO EAT FOR DINNER

Joan got home late from work today, and she was very hungry. When she opened the refrigerator, she was upset. There was nothing to eat for dinner. Joan sat down and made a shopping list. She needed a head of lettuce, a bunch of carrots, a quart of milk, a dozen eggs, two pounds of tomatoes, half a pound of chicken, and a loaf of bread.

Joan rushed out of the house and drove to the supermarket. When she got there, she was very disappointed. There wasn't any lettuce. There weren't any carrots. There wasn't any milk. There weren't any eggs. There weren't any tomatoes. There wasn't any chicken, and there wasn't any bread.

Joan was tired and upset. In fact, she was so tired and upset that she lost her appetite, drove home, didn't have dinner, and went to bed.

✓ READING *CHECK-UP*

Q & A

Joan is at the supermarket. Using these models, create dialogs based on the story.

A. Excuse me. I'm looking for *a head of lettuce.*
B. Sorry. There isn't any more *lettuce.*
A. There isn't?
B. No, there isn't. Sorry.

A. Excuse me. I'm looking for *a bunch of carrots.*
B. Sorry. There aren't any more *carrots.*
A. There aren't?
B. No, there aren't. Sorry.

LISTENING

Listen and choose what the people are talking about.

1. a. chicken   b. milk
2. a. oranges   b. flour
3. a. cookies   b. bread
4. a. potatoes   b. lettuce
5. a. eggs   b. meat
6. a. cereal   b. bananas
7. a. cake   b. soup
8. a. onions   b. soda

What Would You Like?

A. What would you like **for dessert**?

B. I can't decide. What do you recommend?

A. I recommend our **chocolate ice cream**. Everybody says **it's** delicious.*

B. Okay. Please give me **a dish of chocolate ice cream**.

A. What would you like **for breakfast**?

B. I can't decide. What do you recommend?

A. I recommend our **scrambled eggs**. Everybody says **they're** out of this world.*

B. Okay. Please give me **an order of scrambled eggs**.

* delicious / very good / excellent / wonderful / fantastic / magnificent / out of this world

1. for lunch?
   a bowl of

2. for breakfast?
   an order of

3. for dessert?
   a piece of

4. to drink?
   a glass of

5. for dessert?
   a bowl of

6. to drink?
   a cup of

7. for dessert?
   a dish of

8.

How to Say It!

Making a Recommendation About Food

A. What do you recommend for *breakfast*?*

B. I { recommend / suggest } the *pancakes*.

* breakfast / lunch / dinner / dessert

Practice conversations with other students. Ask for and make recommendations.

Stanley's Favorite Recipes

Are you going to have a party soon? Do you want to cook something special? Stanley the chef recommends this recipe for VEGETABLE STEW. Everybody says it's fantastic!

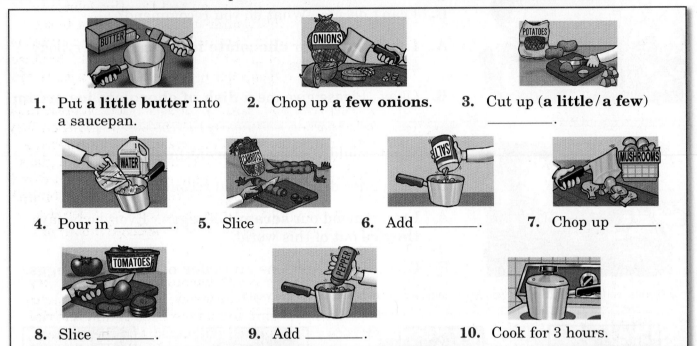

1. Put **a little butter** into a saucepan.

2. Chop up **a few onions**.

3. Cut up (**a little** / **a few**) _____ .

4. Pour in _____ .

5. Slice _____ .

6. Add _____ .

7. Chop up _____ .

8. Slice _____ .

9. Add _____ .

10. Cook for 3 hours.

When is your English teacher's birthday? Do you want to bake a special cake? Stanley the chef recommends this recipe for FRUITCAKE. Everybody says it's out of this world!

1. Put **a few cups of flour** into a mixing bowl.

2. Add **a little sugar**.

3. Slice (**a little** / **a few**) _____ .

4. Cut up _____ .

5. Pour in _____ .

6. Add _____ .

7. Chop up _____ .

8. Add _____ .

9. Mix in _____ .

10. Bake for 45 minutes.

Project

Do you have a favorite recipe? Write the recipe, and share it with other students. Then as a class, put all your recipes together and make a class cookbook.

READING

AT THE CONTINENTAL RESTAURANT

Yesterday was Sherman and Dorothy Johnson's thirty-fifth wedding anniversary. They went to the Continental Restaurant for dinner. This restaurant is a very special place for Sherman and Dorothy because they went there on their first date thirty-six years ago.

Sherman and Dorothy sat at a quiet romantic table in the corner. They looked at the menu, and then they ordered dinner. For an appetizer, Dorothy ordered a bowl of vegetable soup, and Sherman ordered a glass of tomato juice. For the main course, Dorothy ordered baked chicken with rice, and Sherman ordered broiled fish with potatoes. For dessert, Dorothy ordered a piece of apple pie, and Sherman ordered a bowl of strawberries.

Sherman and Dorothy enjoyed their dinner very much. The soup was delicious, and the tomato juice was fresh. The chicken was wonderful, and the rice was tasty. The fish was fantastic, and the potatoes were excellent. The apple pie was magnificent, and the strawberries were out of this world.

Sherman and Dorothy had a wonderful evening at the Continental Restaurant. It was a very special anniversary.

ROLE PLAY

Sherman and Dorothy are ordering dinner from their waiter or waitress. Using these lines to begin, work in groups of three and create a role play based on the story.

  A. Would you like to order now?
  B. Yes. For an appetizer, I'd like . . .
  C. And I'd like . . .

Now, the waiter or waitress is asking about the dinner. Using this model, continue your role play based on all the foods in the story.

  A. How (is / are) the _____?
  B. (It's / They're) _____.
  A. I'm glad you like (it / them).
      And how (is / are) the _____?
  C. (It's / They're) _____.
  A. I'm glad you like (it / them).

25

PRONUNCIATION *Of* Before Consonants and Vowels

Listen. Then say it.

a bowl of soup

a head of lettuce

a piece of apple pie

a bag of onions

Say it. Then listen.

a glass of milk

a jar of jam

a pound of oranges

a dish of ice cream

SIDE by SIDE JOURNAL

In your journal, write about a special meal you enjoyed—in your home, in someone else's home, or at a restaurant. What foods did you have? Who was at the meal? Why was it special?

GRAMMAR FOCUS

COUNT / NON-COUNT NOUNS

Lettuce Butter Milk	is	
		very expensive.
Apples Carrots Onions	are	

Add	a little	salt. sugar. honey.
	a few	potatoes. nuts. raisins.

IMPERATIVES

Please **give me** a dish of ice cream.
Put a little butter into a saucepan.
Cook for 3 hours.

Choose the correct word.

1. Add a (little   few) salt.
2. Cheese (is   are) very expensive this week.
3. Put a (little   few) cups of flour into a bowl.
4. There (isn't   aren't) any more lettuce.
5. Slice a (little   few) tomatoes.
6. The fish (was   were) tasty.
7. The potatoes (was   were) excellent.
8. Chop up a (little   few) nuts.

PARTITIVES

a **bag of** flour
a **bottle of** ketchup
a **box of** cereal
a **bunch of** bananas
a **can of** soup

a **dozen** eggs
a **gallon of** milk
a **half pound (half a pound) of** cheese
a **head of** lettuce

a **jar of** jam
a **loaf of** bread
a **pint of** ice cream
a **pound of** meat
a **quart of** orange juice

a **bowl of** chicken soup
a **cup of** hot chocolate
a **dish of** ice cream
a **glass of** milk
an **order of** scrambled eggs
a **piece of** apple pie

Complete the sentences.

9. I bought a _____ of lettuce.
10. Please get a _____ eggs.
11. We need two _____ of cereal.
12. I'm looking for a _____ of flour.
13. I had a _____ of chicken soup for lunch.
14. He had a _____ of pie for dessert.
15. Please give me an _____ of scrambled eggs.
16. I'd like a _____ of ice cream for dessert, please.

1 CONVERSATION LOCATING ITEMS IN A SUPERMARKET

Practice conversations with a classmate. Use the directory to find the correct section and aisle for these items.

A. Excuse me. Where are the _____?

B. They're in the _____ section, Aisle ____.

A. Thank you.

A. Excuse me. Where's the _____?

B. It's in the _____ section, Aisle ____.

A. Thank you.

STORE DIRECTORY

Section	Aisle
Baked Goods	6
Beverages	4
Dairy	2
Frozen Foods	5
Meat	3
Produce	1

1.
2.
3. POLLY'S ICE CREAM
4.
5.
6.
7.
8.
9.
10.
11.
12.

2 TEAMWORK CATEGORIZING

Bring a supermarket ad to class. Work with a classmate. On a piece of paper, write the names of the six supermarket sections on this page. Then list items in your supermarket ad in the correct section.

READING A SUPERMARKET RECEIPT

```
        SAVE MORE SUPERMARKET
LETTUCE                          1.80
WHOLE WHEAT BREAD                2.50
ORANGE JUICE 1 GAL.             3.19
MILK 1 QT.                       1.29
3 LBS. @ $1.20 LB.
CHICKEN                          3.60
4 @ $1.00
TOMATOES                         4.00
1/2 LB. @ $9.00 LB.
SWISS CHEESE                     4.50
8 @ 4 FOR $1.00
BANANAS                          2.00
...............................
              TOTAL     $22.88
      CASH TENDERED     $25.00
             CHANGE     $ 2.12
```

Look at the receipt and answer the questions.

1. How much is a loaf of whole wheat bread?
   A. $1.80   B. $2.50   C. $1.29

2. How much orange juice did the person buy?
   A. a pound   B. a quart   C. a gallon

3. How much does a pound of chicken cost?
   A. $1.20   B. $3.60   C. $2.00

4. How many tomatoes did the person buy?
   A. three   B. eight   C. four

5. How much do eight bananas cost?
   A. $1.00   B. $2.00   C. $3.00

6. How much does Swiss cheese cost?
   A. 4 for $1.00 B. $4.50 a pound C. $9.00 a pound

Now find the answers to these questions. Circle the answers on the receipt.

1. How many pounds of chicken did the person buy?
2. How much does a head of lettuce cost?
3. How much Swiss cheese did the person buy?
4. How much milk did the person buy?
5. How much did the person pay for tomatoes?
6. How much did the person spend today?

READING A FOOD LABEL

COLUMBUS LOW FAT MILK 1% Milk Fat
Nutrition Facts
Serving Size 1 cup (240mL)
Servings per Container 4

Amount per Serving	
Calories 110	Calories from Fat 20
	% Daily Value
Total Fat 3g	4%
Cholesterol 10mg	4%
Sodium 130 mg	5%
Total Carbohydrate 13mg	4%
Vitamin A 10% • Vitamin C	4%
Calcium 30% • Vitamin D	25%

Keep Refrigerated

Read the label. Decide if the following sentences are True (T) or False (F).

_____ 1. This milk doesn't have any fat.

_____ 2. There are four cups of milk in the container.

_____ 3. A cup of this milk has four grams of fat.

_____ 4. This milk contains three types of vitamins.

_____ 5. You can put this milk in your kitchen cabinet.

_____ 6. This milk has more fat than regular milk.

TEAMWORK Bring a supermarket receipt and a food label to class. Work with a classmate. Ask each other questions about your receipts and labels.

Look at the menu and answer the questions.

Annie's Place

Soups
Chicken Soup	Cup	$2.25
	Bowl	$3.00
Mushroom Soup	Cup	$2.50
	Bowl	$3.50

Salads
Greek Salad	Small	$3.00
	Large	$4.25
Chef's Salad		$3.50
with chicken		$5.00

Sandwiches
Chicken Salad	$4.00
Egg Salad	$2.75
Cheese	$2.50
Hamburger	$4.50

served with lettuce, tomato, and french fries

Lunch Specials
Baked Chicken	$10.00

served with rice and choice of vegetable
Broiled Fish of the Day	$12.00

served with any two side dishes
Spaghetti with Annie's Tomato Sauce	$6.50

served with salad and choice of vegetable
with meatballs	$8.50

Side Dishes ($1.50 each)
Baked Potato   French Fries   Rice
Mushrooms   Carrots   Green Beans

Beverages
Soda	$1.50	Coffee	$2.00
Juice	$2.00	Tea	$1.50

Desserts
Chocolate Cake $3.50   Apple Pie $4.00

1. A bowl of chicken soup and a cheese sandwich cost ___.
A. $5.50 B. $6.00 C. $6.25 D. $6.50

2. A cup of chicken soup and a large Greek salad cost ___.
A. $6.00 B. $6.25 C. $6.50 D. $7.25

3. A hamburger comes with ___.
A. soup B. salad C. soda D. french fries

4. A chicken salad sandwich with french fries and a glass of juice costs ___.
A. $6.50 B. $7.50 C. $8.00 D. $8.50

5. When you order baked chicken with rice and green beans you pay ___.
A. $10.00 B. $11.50 C. $12.00 D. $13.00

6. Roberto only has two dollars. He can order ___.
A. a salad B. a sandwich C. soup D. a beverage

7. Spaghetti and meatballs, a cup of tea, and a piece of apple pie cost ___.
A. $13.00 B. $13.50 C. $14.00 D. $15.00

8. Broiled fish does NOT come with ___.
A. carrots B. salad C. rice D. a baked potato

9. A chef's salad with chicken, a glass of soda, and a piece of chocolate cake cost ___.
A. $8.50 B. $9.50 C. $10.00 D. $12.50

10. Baked chicken comes with rice and any ___.
A. beverage B. dessert C. salad D. side dish

TEAMWORK Bring a restaurant menu to class. Work with a classmate. Ask each other questions about the food and the prices on the menus.

Choose the correct answer.

1. I ordered a ___ for dessert.
A. bowl of soup
B. bag of flour
C. piece of pie
D. loaf of bread

2. I'm slicing some ___.
A. tomatoes
B. sugar
C. soup
D. juice

3. I recommend our ___ for breakfast.
A. flour
B. chocolate ice cream
C. lettuce
D. pancakes

4. Next, chop up some ___.
A. jam
B. nuts
C. flour
D. milk

5. The recipe says to pour in some ___.
A. fish
B. bread
C. cheese
D. water

6. Oranges are in the ___ section.
A. Produce
B. Dairy
C. Meat
D. Beverages

Look at the supermarket receipt. Choose the correct answer.

7. The person bought ___ of milk.
A. a pint
B. a quart
C. a gallon
D. a pound

8. A pound of fish costs ___.
A. $2.00
B. $7.00
C. $8.00
D. $14.00

9. The person bought ___.
A. a pound of cheese
B. seven pounds of fish
C. six onions
D. six lemons

10. The person spent ___.
A. $32.03
B. $7.97
C. $40.00
D. $47.97

```
BUY & SAVE SUPERMARKET
         * * *
WHITE BREAD           2.20
SUGAR                 1.80
MILK 1 GAL.           3.10
ORANGE JUICE 1 QT.    1.63
2 LBS @ $7.00 LB.
FISH                 14.00
3 @ $1.10
ONIONS                3.30
1/2 LB.@ $8.00 LB.
CHEESE                4.00
6 @ 3 FOR $1.00
LEMONS                2.00
                   --------
            TOTAL   $32.03
    CASH TENDERED   $40.00
           CHANGE  $ 7.97
```

SKILLS CHECK ✔

Words:
☐ apple
☐ apple pie
☐ baked chicken
☐ baking soda
☐ banana
☐ bread
☐ broiled fish
☐ carrot
☐ cereal
☐ cheese
☐ chicken
☐ eggs
☐ flour
☐ grapes
☐ honey
☐ hot chocolate

☐ ice cream
☐ jam
☐ ketchup
☐ lettuce
☐ meat
☐ milk
☐ mushrooms
☐ nuts
☐ onions
☐ orange juice
☐ pancakes
☐ raisins
☐ scrambled eggs
☐ soda
☐ soup
☐ strawberries

☐ sugar
☐ Swiss cheese
☐ tomato juice
☐ tomatoes
☐ vanilla ice cream
☐ water
☐ white bread
☐ whole wheat bread

☐ Baked Goods
☐ Beverages
☐ Dairy
☐ Frozen Foods
☐ Meat
☐ Produce

I can ask & answer:
☐ How much does *a head of lettuce* cost?
☐ What would you like for *dessert*?
☐ What do you recommend for *breakfast*?
☐ Excuse me. Where are the *apples*?

I can:
☐ identify supermarket sections
☐ interpret a supermarket receipt
☐ read a food label
☐ order from a restaurant menu

I can write:
☐ a shopping list
☐ recipe instructions

I can write about:
☐ a meal I enjoyed

26d

BUILD YOUR VOCABULARY!

Ordering Fast Food

Food Shopping

Everybody eats, and everybody shops for food!

In the past, people shopped for fruits, vegetables, bread, and meat at small food stores and at open markets. Before there were refrigerators, it was difficult to keep food fresh for a long time, so people shopped almost every day.

Life today is very different from the past. Refrigerators keep food fresh so people don't have to shop every day. People also have very busy lives. They have time to shop for food only once or twice a week.

People shop for food in different kinds of places—in small grocery stores, at large supermarkets, and sometimes at enormous wholesale stores that sell food and other items at very low prices. Some people even shop on the Internet. They order food online, and the company delivers it to their home. And in many places around the world, people still shop in little food stores and at open markets. There are certainly many different ways to shop for food these days!

FACT FILE

One Day's Food

Eggs: The world's hens produce more than 2 billion eggs a day—enough eggs to make an omelet the size of the island of Cyprus!

Chocolate: The world produces 8,818 tons of cocoa beans every day—enough to make 700 million chocolate bars!

Rice: The world produces 1.6 million tons of rice every day—an amount the size of Egypt's Great Pyramid!

I'd like _____ , please.

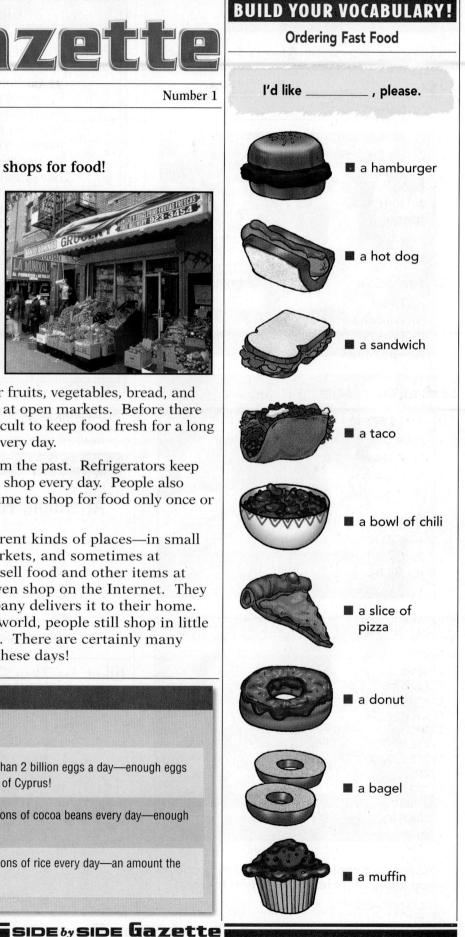

- a hamburger
- a hot dog
- a sandwich
- a taco
- a bowl of chili
- a slice of pizza
- a donut
- a bagel
- a muffin

AROUND THE WORLD

Where People Shop for Food

People in different places shop for food in different ways.

These people shop for food at an open market.

This person buys a fresh loaf of bread every day at this bakery.

These people go to a big supermarket once a week.

Where do people shop for food in countries you know? Where do YOU shop for food?

Global Exchange

Glen25: Hi, Maria. How are you today? I just had breakfast. I had a glass of orange juice, a bowl of cereal, and a muffin. At 12 noon I'm going to have lunch. For lunch I usually have a sandwich and a glass of milk. Our family's big meal of the day is dinner. We usually eat at about 6 P.M. We usually have meat, chicken, or fish, rice or potatoes, and vegetables. How about you? When do you usually eat? What do you have? What's your big meal of the day?

MariaV: Hi, Glen. It's the middle of the afternoon here. Our family just had our big meal of the day. Today we had meat, potatoes, and vegetables. For breakfast I usually have a roll and a cup of hot chocolate. We don't have a big dinner in the evening. We usually have a snack early in the evening and a light supper at about 9:30.

Send a message to a keypal. Tell about the meals you eat.

LISTENING

Attention, Food Shoppers!

_d_	① cereal	**a.**	$2.75
___	② bread	**b.**	$ .40
___	③ orange juice	**c.**	$3.25
___	④ ice cream	**d.**	$3.49
___	⑤ bananas	**e.**	$1.79

What Are They Saying?

4

Future Tense: Will
Time Expressions
Might

- Telling About the Future
- Probability
- Possibility
- Warnings

- Social Interaction: Offers and Invitations
- Reading and Writing Invitations
- Cross-Cultural Expectations
- Reading Skill: Signal Words

VOCABULARY PREVIEW

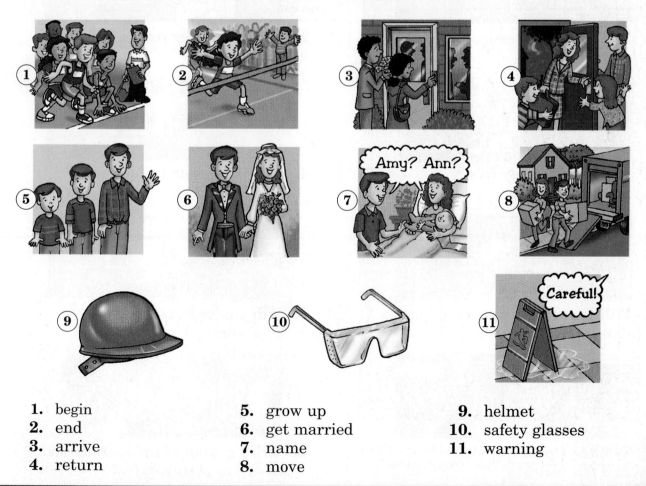

1. begin
2. end
3. arrive
4. return
5. grow up
6. get married
7. name
8. move
9. helmet
10. safety glasses
11. warning

Will the Train Arrive Soon?

(I will)	I'll	
(He will)	He'll	
(She will)	She'll	
(It will)	It'll	work.
(We will)	We'll	
(You will)	You'll	
(They will)	They'll	

Will he work?
Yes, he will.

A. Will the train arrive soon?

B. Yes, it will. It'll arrive in five minutes.

1. Will the game begin soon?
at 7:00

2. Will Ms. Lopez return soon?
in an hour

3. Will you be ready soon?
in a few minutes

4. Will the guests be here soon?
in half an hour

5. Will your brother get home soon?
in a little while

6. Will you be back soon?
in a week

7. Will the storm end soon?
in a few hours

8. Will I get out of the hospital soon?
in two or three days

What Do You Think?

| I / He / She / It / We / You / They | will work. |

| I / He / She / It / We / You / They | won't work. (will not) |

Do you think it'll rain tomorrow?

Maybe it will, and maybe it won't. We'll just have to wait and see.

1. Do you think Mr. Lee will give us a test tomorrow?

2. Do you think your daughter will get married soon?

3. Do you think your parents will move to Florida?

4. Do you think it'll be very cold this winter?

5. Do you think we'll have to work this weekend?

6. Do you think you'll be happy in your new neighborhood?

7. Do you think I'll be famous some day?

8. Do you think there will be many people at the beach tomorrow?

9. Do you think _____?

31

I CAN'T WAIT FOR SPRING TO COME!

I'm tired of winter. I'm tired of snow, I'm tired of cold weather, and I'm sick and tired of winter coats and boots! Just think! In a few more weeks it won't be winter any more. It'll be spring. The weather won't be cold. It'll be warm. It won't snow any more. It'll be sunny. I won't have to stay indoors any more. I'll go outside and play with my friends. We'll ride bicycles and play baseball again.

In a few more weeks our neighborhood won't look sad and gray any more. The flowers will bloom, and the trees will become green again. My family will spend more time outdoors. My father will work in the yard. He'll cut the grass and paint the fence. My mother will work in the yard, too. She'll buy new flowers and plant them in the garden. On weekends we won't just sit in the living room and watch TV. We'll go for walks in the park, and we'll have picnics on Sunday afternoons.

I can't wait for spring to come! Hurry, spring!

✔ READING CHECK-UP

TRUE, FALSE, OR MAYBE?

Answer True, False, or Maybe (if the answer isn't in the story).

1. It's spring.
2. The boy in the story likes to go outside during the spring.
3. The boy has a cold.
4. The trees are green now.
5. The park is near their house.
6. The boy plays baseball with his friends all year.
7. The family has a TV in their living room.
8. The boy's family doesn't like winter.

How About You?

What's your favorite season—spring? summer? fall? winter? Why? What's the weather like in your favorite season? What do you like to do?

They Really Can't Decide

I
He
She
It
We
You
They

} might clean it today.

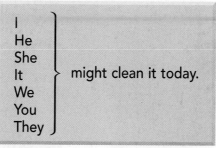

A. When are you going to clean your apartment?

B. I don't know. I might clean it today, or I might clean it next Saturday. I really can't decide.

A. Where are you going to go for your vacation?

B. We don't know. We might go to Mexico, or we might go to Japan. We really can't decide.

1. What's he going to make for dinner tonight?

2. What color is she going to paint her bedroom?

3. What are they going to name their new daughter?

4. When are you two going to get married?

5. What are you going to buy your brother for his birthday?

6. What are they going to do tonight?

7. How are you going to get to school tomorrow?

8. What's he going to name his new puppy?

9. What are you going to be when you grow up?

Careful!

A. Careful! Put on your helmet!

B. I'm sorry. What did you say?

A. Put on your helmet! You might hurt your head.

B. Oh. Thanks for the warning.

1. Put on your safety glasses!
hurt your eyes

2. Don't stand there!
get hit

3. Watch your step!
fall

4. Don't touch that machine!
get hurt

5. Don't touch those wires!
get a shock

6.

How to Say It!

Asking for Repetition

A. *Careful! Watch your step!*

B. I'm sorry.
{ What did you say?
  Could you please repeat that?
  Could you say that again? }

Practice some conversations on this page again. Ask for repetition in different ways.

I'm Afraid I Might Drown

A. Would you like to go swimming with me?

B. No, I don't think so.

A. Why not?

B. I'm afraid I might drown.

A. Don't worry! You won't drown.

B. Are you sure?

A. I'm positive!

B. Okay. I'll go swimming with you.

1. *go skiing*
break my leg

2. *go to the beach*
get a sunburn

3. *go dancing*
step on your feet

4. *take a walk in the park*
catch a cold

5. *go to the movies*
fall asleep

6. *go to the company picnic*
have a terrible time

7. *go on the roller coaster*
get sick

8. *go sailing*
get seasick

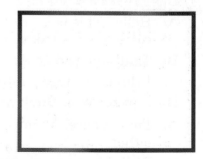

9.

JUST IN CASE

Larry didn't go to work today, and he might not go to work tomorrow either. He might see his doctor instead. He's feeling absolutely terrible, and he thinks he might have the flu. Larry isn't positive, but he doesn't want to take any chances. He thinks it might be a good idea for him to see his doctor . . . just in case.

Mrs. Randall didn't go to the office today, and she might not go to the office tomorrow either. She might go to the doctor instead. She feels nauseous every morning, and she thinks she might be pregnant. Mrs. Randall isn't positive, but she doesn't want to take any chances. She thinks it might be a good idea for her to go to the doctor . . . just in case.

Tommy and Julie Harris didn't go to school today, and they might not go to school tomorrow either. They might stay home in bed instead. They have little red spots all over their arms and legs. Mr. and Mrs. Harris think their children might have the measles. They aren't positive, but they don't want to take any chances. They think it might be a good idea for Tommy and Julie to stay home in bed . . . just in case.

✔ **READING** *CHECK-UP*

CHOOSE

Larry is "calling in sick." Choose the correct words and then practice the conversation.

A. Hello. This is Larry Parker. I'm afraid I (might   can't)[1] come to work today. I think I (will   might)[2] have the flu.

B. That's too bad. (Are you   Will you)[3] going to see your doctor?

A. I think I (might   sure).[4]

B. (Not   Will)[5] you be at work tomorrow?

A. I'm not sure. I (might not   might)[6] go to work tomorrow either.

B. Well, I hope you feel better soon.

A. Thank you.

LISTENING

WHAT'S THE LINE?

Mrs. Harris (from the story on page 36) is calling Tommy and Julie's school. Listen and choose the correct lines.

1. a. Hello. This is Mrs. Harris.
   b. Hello. This is the Park Elementary School.
2. a. I can't.
   b. Tommy and Julie won't be in school today.
3. a. They might have the measles.
   b. Yes. This is their mother.
4. a. They aren't bad. They're just sick.
   b. Yes.
5. a. Thank you.
   b. It might be a good idea.

Good morning. Park Elementary School.

WHAT'S THE WORD?

Listen and choose the word you hear.

1. a. can't   b. might
2. a. want to   b. won't
3. a. here   b. there
4. a. we'll   b. will
5. a. they'll   b. they
6. a. hurt   b. hit
7. a. I   b. I'll
8. a. red   b. wet
9. a. sick   b. seasick

Write a Note!

Your child didn't go to school yesterday. Write a note to the teacher and explain why.

..........., 20......

Dear ....,

.... didn't go to school yesterday because

....

....

Sincerely,

....

PRONUNCIATION *Going to*

going to = gonna

Listen. Then say it.

When are you going to
  clean your room?
What color is she going to
  paint her bedroom?
How are they going to get
  to school?

Say it. Then listen.

When are you going to
  get married?
What's he going to name
  his cat?
When am I going to get
  out of the hospital?

SIDE by SIDE JOURNAL

Write in your journal about your future. Where do you think you might live? Where do you think you might work? What do you think might happen in your life?

GRAMMAR FOCUS

FUTURE TENSE: WILL

(I will)	I'll	
(He will)	He'll	
(She will)	She'll	
(It will)	It'll	work.
(We will)	We'll	
(You will)	You'll	
(They will)	They'll	

I	
He	
She	
It	won't work.
We	
You	
They	

	I	
	he	
	she	
Will	it	arrive soon?
	we	
	you	
	they	

	I	
	he	
	she	
Yes,	it	will.
	we	
	you	
	they	

	I	
	he	
	she	
No,	it	won't.
	we	
	you	
	they	

TIME EXPRESSIONS

		a few	days. minutes. hours. weeks. months.
The train will arrive	in		a week. an hour. half an hour. a little while. two or three days.
	at seven o'clock.		

MIGHT

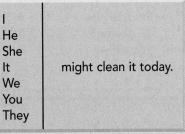

I	
He	
She	
It	might clean it today.
We	
You	
They	

Complete the sentences.

1. A. _____ Mrs. Sanchez return soon?
   B. Yes, _____ _____. _____ return in an hour.

2. A. _____ the flowers bloom soon?
   B. Yes, _____ _____. _____ bloom in a week.

3. A. _____ there be many people at the party tonight?
   B. No, _____ _____.

4. A. _____ you call me today?
   B. Yes, _____ _____. _____ call you soon.

5. A. _____ your brother be ready soon?
   B. No, _____ _____. He's still sleeping.

6. A. _____ you and your wife visit us soon?
   B. Yes, _____ _____. _____ visit you on Sunday.

7. A. Do you think it _____ be a nice day tomorrow?
   B. Maybe _____ _____, and maybe _____ _____.

8. A. Do you think _____ catch a cold?
   B. No, you _____. _____ be fine.

38

1 CONVERSATION MAKING, ACCEPTING, & DECLINING OFFERS

Practice the conversations with a classmate.

A. Would you like some french fries?

B. Yes. Thanks.

Now work with other classmates.
Practice making, accepting, and declining offers.

A. Would you like some more coffee?

B. No, thank you.

A. Would you like _____?

B. { Yes. Thanks.
No, thank you.

2 CONVERSATION MAKING, ACCEPTING, & DECLINING INVITATIONS

Practice the conversations with a classmate.

A. Would you like to have dinner with my family tomorrow?

B. Yes. I'd love to.

Now work with other classmates.
Practice making, accepting, and declining invitations.

A. Would you like to go out for lunch today?

B. I'm sorry. I can't. I have to work.

A. Would you like to _____?

B. { Yes. I'd love to.
I'm sorry. I can't. I have to _____.

Look at the invitations and answer the questions.

IT'S A SURPRISE!
Shhh! "Keep it under your hat!"

Please join us as we celebrate
Mark Lane's 30th Birthday!

Sunday, March 5th
at Jeffrey Wagner's house
725 Garfield Street, Silverton

Be there at 6 P.M. Don't be late!

There will be hot dogs, hamburgers, and beverages for all. Please bring an appetizer, a side dish, or dessert.

RSVP before March 1st by e-mail only
jwagner@worldmail.com

Mr. and Mrs. Alberto Velez
request the honor of your presence
at the wedding of their daughter

Susanna Rose
to
Richard Hansen

son of Mr. Martin Hansen and Ms. Lena Grant

on Saturday, October thirtieth,
two thousand and ten

at six thirty in the evening

at Saint Mark's Church
Seventeen Ivy Lane
Rosedale, New York

Reception following the ceremony at
The Candlelight Inn
Twenty Fuller Road
Rosedale, New York

1. The birthday invitation is from _____.
   A. Mr. and Mrs. Velez
   B. Jeffrey Wagner
   C. Mark Lane

2. Guests can bring _____ to the birthday party.
   A. hot dogs or hamburgers
   B. cookies or ice cream
   C. juice or soda

3. You need to answer the birthday invitation _____.
   A. before 6 o'clock
   B. after March fifth
   C. by e-mail

4. "Keep it under your hat" means _____.
   A. don't tell Mark Lane about the party
   B. wear a hat to the birthday party
   C. put the birthday invitation in a hat

5. The wedding ceremony is _____.
   A. at the Candlelight Inn
   B. at Saint Mark's Church
   C. on Saturday, October 13, 2010

6. _____ are getting married.
   A. Mr. and Mrs. Alberto Velez
   B. Mr. Martin Hansen and Ms. Lena Grant
   C. Susanna Rose Velez and Richard Hansen

7. The reception is _____.
   A. at six thirty in the evening
   B. after the wedding ceremony
   C. at 17 Ivy Lane

8. "Mr. and Mrs. Velez request the honor of your presence" means _____.
   A. Mr. and Mrs. Velez invite you to come
   B. please reply to this invitation
   C. Mr. and Mrs. Velez thank you for your gifts

WRITING Your Invitation You're inviting the students in your class to a party. What kind of party are you having? When is the party? Where is it going to be? Make an invitation.

Dinner Invitations Around the World

Some friends invited you to their home for dinner. When should you arrive? How much should you eat? When should you leave? The answers to these questions depend on the country you're in. Different countries have different rules and traditions.

In the United States, punctuality (being on time) is very important. When people invite you to their home for dinner, they usually give an exact time, for example, "We're having dinner at 6:30." You should plan to arrive on time or just a little late. If you're going to be more than fifteen minutes late, you need to call. Punctuality is also important in Sweden, Norway, and other Scandinavian countries. However, in countries in South America and in Italy and Spain, a guest can arrive half an hour late for a dinner invitation. In most countries, it isn't a good idea to arrive early in case the hosts who are making the dinner aren't ready for their guests.

Food is a very important part of any invitation to someone's home in the countries of the Middle East.

When someone offers you something to eat or drink, it's impolite to say "no". But you don't have to finish everything. In fact, when your plate is empty, your host will serve you more right away. So when you're full, stop eating and leave something on your plate. This is very different from France, Austria, and Japan, where it's important to finish everything on your plate to show your host that you liked the food. In Italy and Turkey, you don't have to finish everything, but if you do and you're still hungry, it's polite to ask for more.

It's important to know when to arrive for dinner, but it's also important to know when to leave! In India, Europe, and North America, it's very impolite to leave right after you eat. You don't want your hosts to think that you came to their home only for the food. On the other hand, in some Asian and Central American countries, it's polite to leave right after dessert. If you stay, the hosts might think you're still hungry and there wasn't enough food.

1. It's important to be on time in _____.
   A. Italy
   B. Spain
   C. Norway
   D. Brazil

2. It's polite to leave right after dinner in some countries in _____.
   A. Europe
   B. North America
   C. Scandinavia
   D. Central America

3. When dinner is at 7:30 P.M. in the United States, it's polite to arrive _____.
   A. more than fifteen minutes late
   B. at 7:40 P.M.
   C. at 7:50 P.M.
   D. at 7:15 P.M.

4. _____ is a Scandinavian country.
   A. India
   B. The United States
   C. Sweden
   D. Austria

5. Finish everything on your plate in _____, or your host will think you don't like the food.
   A. Austria
   B. Italy
   C. Turkey
   D. the Middle East

6. According to this article, in the Middle East, it's important to _____.
   A. be on time
   B. leave right after dinner
   C. eat everything on your plate
   D. say "yes" when someone offers food

Reading Tip

Signal words can help you understand the information in a reading. In this article, the author uses the words *however*, *but*, and *on the other hand* to show differences between information before these words and after them. Find these words in the reading. What differences do they help to show?

Choose the correct answer.

1. The ____ will arrive in fifteen minutes.
   A. game
   B. train
   C. vacation
   D. measles

2. Remember to put on your ____.
   A. warning
   B. floor
   C. helmet
   D. feet

3. We're going on vacation. We'll be back ____.
   A. in a few minutes
   B. this afternoon
   C. in half an hour
   D. in a week

4. Don't touch that wire! You might ____.
   A. get a shock
   B. see your doctor
   C. get seasick
   D. drown

5. I'm going to call the doctor. I think my son might ____.
   A. bloom
   B. be sick and tired of the weather
   C. have the flu
   D. be famous

6. Watch your step! You might ____.
   A. fall asleep
   B. fall
   C. catch a cold
   D. get sick

7. ____ I can't have dinner with you tomorrow.
   A. I have to.
   B. I'd love to.
   C. I'm sorry.
   D. Yes. Thanks.

8. I received ____ to a wedding.
   A. an invitation
   B. a ceremony
   C. a reception
   D. a surprise

9. My friends ____ me to their home for dinner.
   A. arrived
   B. wanted
   C. returned
   D. invited

10. Dinner is almost ready. Will our guests ____ soon?
    A. get home
    B. be here
    C. get out
    D. end

SKILLS CHECK ✓

Words:
- □ arrive
- □ be back
- □ begin
- □ end
- □ get home
- □ return
- □ break *my* leg
- □ catch a cold
- □ fall
- □ get a shock
- □ get a sunburn
- □ get hit
- □ get hurt
- □ get seasick
- □ get sick
- □ hurt *your* head/eyes
- □ the flu
- □ the measles
- □ celebrate
- □ get married
- □ grow up
- □ move
- □ name (v)
- □ ceremony
- □ reception
- □ RSVP

I can ask & answer:
- □ Will I/we/you/they/he/she/it *be back soon*?
- □ Do you think I/we/you/they/he/she/it will *be back soon*?

I can ask for repetition:
- □ I'm sorry. What did you say?
- □ I'm sorry. Could you please repeat that?
- □ I'm sorry. Could you say that again?

I can make, accept, & decline an offer:
- □ Would you like *some french fries*?
  Yes. Thanks.
  No, thank you.

I can make, accept, & decline an invitation:
- □ Would you like to *go out for lunch*?
  Yes. I'd love to.
  I'm sorry. I can't. I have to *work*.

I can write:
- □ a note to a teacher to explain a child's absence from school
- □ a story about my future
- □ an invitation to a party

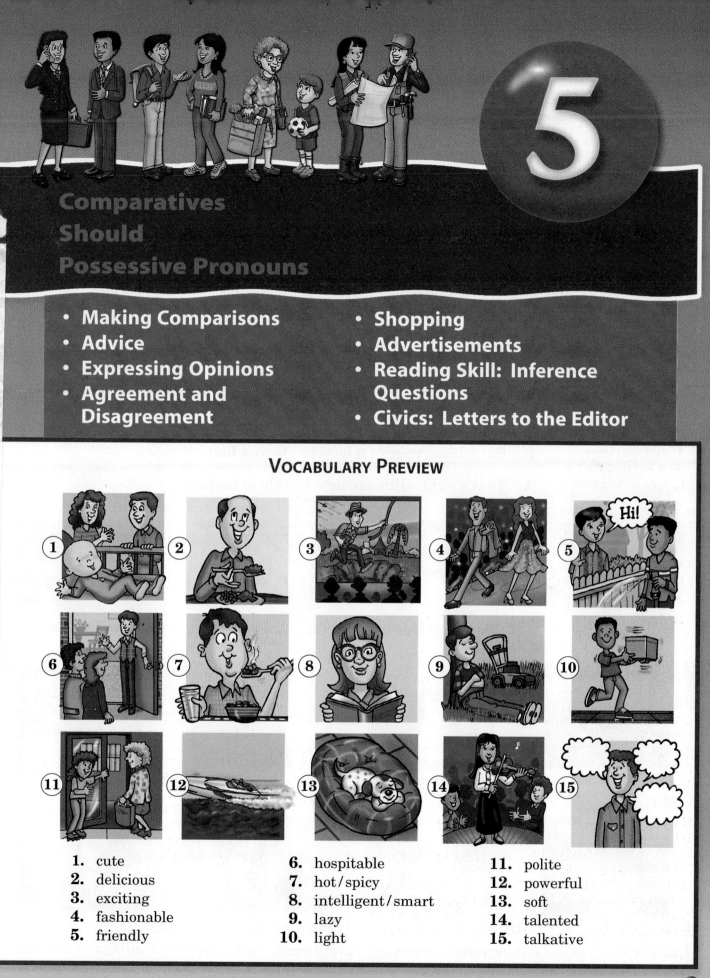

5

Comparatives
Should
Possessive Pronouns

- **Making Comparisons**
- **Advice**
- **Expressing Opinions**
- **Agreement and Disagreement**

- **Shopping**
- **Advertisements**
- **Reading Skill: Inference Questions**
- **Civics: Letters to the Editor**

VOCABULARY PREVIEW

1. cute
2. delicious
3. exciting
4. fashionable
5. friendly
6. hospitable
7. hot / spicy
8. intelligent / smart
9. lazy
10. light
11. polite
12. powerful
13. soft
14. talented
15. talkative

My New Bicycle Is Faster

| soft – softer
small – smaller | large – larger
safe – safer | big – bigger
hot – hotter | fancy – fancier
pretty – prettier |

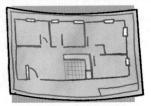

A. I think you'll like my new bicycle.

B. But I liked your OLD bicycle. It was **fast**.

A. That's right. But my new bicycle is **faster**.

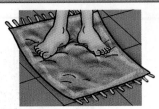

1. *rug*
   soft

2. *tennis racket*
   light

3. *apartment*
   large

4. *neighborhood*
   safe

5. *office*
   big

6. *recipe for chili*
   hot

7. *dog*
   friendly

8. *sports car*
   fancy

9. *dishwasher*
   quiet

10. *wig*
    pretty

11. *cell phone*
    small

12. *cat*
    cute

My New Rocking Chair Is More Comfortable

fast – faster
nice – nicer
big – bigger
pretty – prettier

comfortable – more comfortable
beautiful – more beautiful
interesting – more interesting
intelligent – more intelligent

A. I think you'll like my new rocking chair.

B. But I liked your OLD rocking chair. It was **comfortable**.

A. That's right. But my new rocking chair is **more comfortable**.

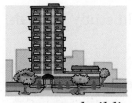

1. *apartment building*
beautiful

2. *roommate*
interesting

3. *girlfriend*
intelligent

4. *boyfriend*
handsome

5. *briefcase*
attractive

6. *computer*
powerful

7. *printer*
fast

8. *English teacher*
smart

9. *recipe for meatloaf*
delicious

10. *boss*
nice

11. *parrot*
talkative

12.

Bicycles Are Safer Than Motorcycles

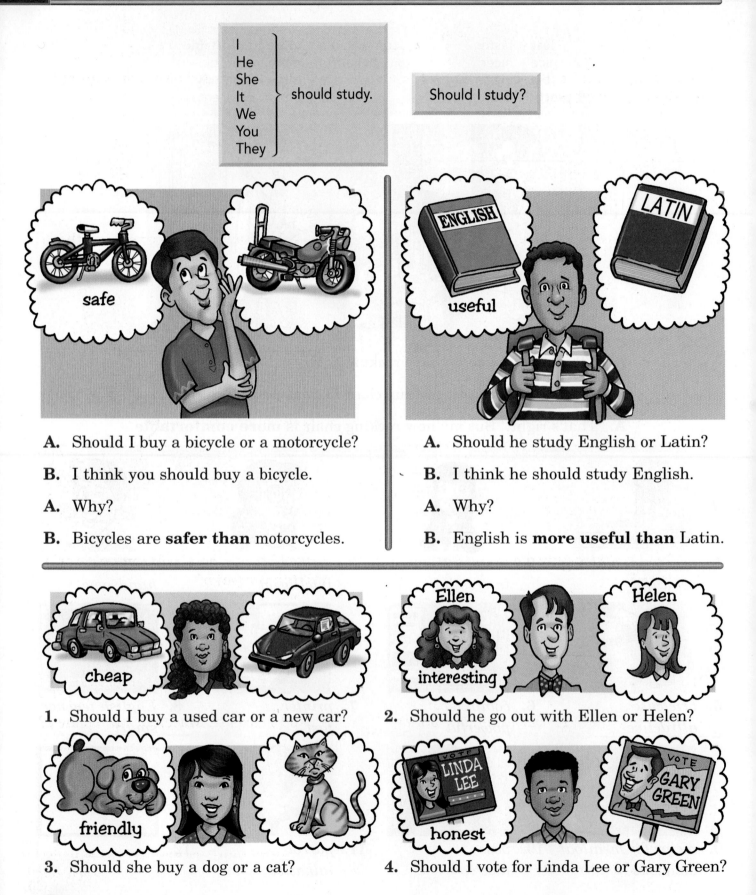

I
He
She
It
We
You
They
} should study.

Should I study?

safe

useful

A. Should I buy a bicycle or a motorcycle?

B. I think you should buy a bicycle.

A. Why?

B. Bicycles are **safer than** motorcycles.

A. Should he study English or Latin?

B. I think he should study English.

A. Why?

B. English is **more useful than** Latin.

cheap

Ellen
interesting

Helen

1. Should I buy a used car or a new car?

2. Should he go out with Ellen or Helen?

friendly

LINDA LEE

honest

VOTE GARY GREEN

3. Should she buy a dog or a cat?

4. Should I vote for Linda Lee or Gary Green?

5. Should she take a course with Professor Blake or Professor Drake?

6. Should they plant flowers or vegetables this spring?

7. Should we buy this fan or that fan?

8. Should she buy these earrings or those earrings?

9. Should he take piano lessons with Mrs. Clark or Miss Smith?

10. Should I buy the hat in my left hand or the hat in my right hand?

11. Should she buy fur gloves or leather gloves?

12. Should I buy a notebook computer or a desktop computer?

13. Should I hire Ms. Parker or Ms. Jones?

14. Should I fire Mr. Mason or Mr. Grimes?

15. Should we rent this movie or that movie?

16.

READING

IT ISN'T EASY BEING A TEENAGER

I try to be a good son, but no matter how hard I try, my parents never seem to be satisfied. They think I should be a better* son. They think I should eat healthier food, I should wear nicer clothes, and I should get better grades. And according to them, my hair should be shorter, my room should be neater, and my friends should be more polite when they come to visit.

You know . . . it isn't easy being a teenager.

IT ISN'T EASY BEING PARENTS

We try to be good parents, but no matter how hard we try, our children never seem to be satisfied. They think we should be better parents. They think we should wear more fashionable clothes, we should drive a newer car, and we should listen to more interesting music. And according to them, we should be more sympathetic when they talk about their problems, we should be friendlier when their friends come to visit, and we should be more understanding when they come home late on Saturday night.

You know . . . it isn't easy being parents.

* good – better

✔ READING *CHECK-UP*

WHAT'S THE WORD?

According to this boy's parents, he doesn't eat __healthy__ ¹ food, he doesn't wear _____² clothes, he doesn't get _____³ grades, his hair isn't _____⁴, and his friends aren't _____⁵ when they come to visit.

According to their children, these parents don't wear _____⁶ clothes, they don't have a _____⁷ car, they don't listen to _____⁸ music, and they aren't _____⁹ when their children's friends come to visit.

LISTENING

Listen and choose what the people are talking about.

1. a. TV   b. printer
2. a. chair   b. recipe
3. a. hair   b. apartment
4. a. offices   b. friends
5. a. neighborhood   b. briefcase
6. a. rug   b. computer

Don't Be Ridiculous!

A. You know, my dog isn't as friendly as your dog.

B. Don't be ridiculous! Yours is MUCH friendlier than **mine**.

A. You know, my novels aren't as interesting as Ernest Hemingway's novels.

B. Don't be ridiculous! Yours are MUCH more interesting than **his**.

clean

powerful

nice

1. *my apartment*
   your apartment

2. *my computer*
   Bob's computer

3. *my boss*
   your boss

comfortable

big

She sells sea shells...
good

4. *my furniture*
   your furniture

5. *my house*
   the Jacksons' house

6. *my pronunciation*
   Maria's pronunciation

pretty

FRUITCAKE
delicious

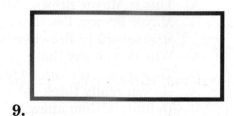

7. *my garden*
   your garden

8. *my recipe for fruitcake*
   Stanley's recipe for fruitcake

9.

BROWNSVILLE

The Taylor family lived in Brownsville for many years. And for many years, Brownsville was a very good place to live. The streets were clean, the parks were safe, the bus system was reliable, and the schools were good.

But Brownsville changed. Today the streets aren't as clean as they used to be. The parks aren't as safe as they used to be. The bus system isn't as reliable as it used to be. And the schools aren't as good as they used to be.

Because of the changes in Brownsville, the Taylor family moved to Newport last year. In Newport the streets are cleaner, the parks are safer, the bus system is more reliable, and the schools are better. The Taylors are happy in Newport, but they were happier in Brownsville. Although Newport has cleaner streets, safer parks, a more reliable bus system, and better schools, Brownsville has friendlier people. They're nicer, more polite, and more hospitable than the people in Newport.

The Taylors miss Brownsville. Even though they're now living in Newport, Brownsville will always be their real home.

✔ READING CHECK-UP

Q & A

The people of Brownsville are calling Mayor Brown's radio talk show. They're upset about Brownsville's streets, parks, bus system, and schools. Using this model and the story, call Mayor Brown.

A. This is Mayor Brown. You're on the air.
B. Mayor Brown, I'm very upset about the *streets* here in Brownsville.
A. Why do you say that?
B. *They aren't* as *clean* as *they* used to be.
A. Do you really think so?
B. Definitely! You know . . . they say the *streets* in Newport *are cleaner*.
A. I'll see what I can do. Thank you for calling.

Agreeing & Disagreeing

A. { I think . . .
    { In my opinion, . . .

B. { I agree.
    { I agree with you.
    { I think so, too.

C. { I disagree.
    { I disagree with you.
    { I don't think so.

Practice interactions on this page, using these expressions for agreeing and disagreeing.

INTERACTIONS

_____er } than
more _____

as _____ as
not as _____ as

I think New York is more interesting than Los Angeles.

I disagree. I think Los Angeles is MUCH more interesting than New York.

In my opinion, the weather in Honolulu is better than the weather in Miami.

I don't think so. I think the weather in Miami is better than the weather in Honolulu.

In my opinion, the people in Centerville aren't as friendly as the people in Greenville.

I agree. But the people in Centerville are more interesting.

I think so, too.

**Practice conversations with other students. Compare different places you know.
Talk about . . .**

the streets (*quiet, safe, clean, wide, busy*)
the buildings (*tall, modern, attractive*)
the weather (*cold, cool, warm, hot, rainy, snowy*)
the people (*friendly, nice, polite, honest, happy, hospitable, talkative, healthy*)
the city in general (*large, interesting, exciting, expensive*)

PRONUNCIATION Yes / No Questions with *or*

Listen. Then say it.

Should I buy a bicycle or a motorcycle?

Should we buy this fan or that fan?

Should he go out with Ellen or Helen?

Should she buy fur gloves or leather gloves?

Say it. Then listen.

Should they plant flowers or vegetables?

Should she buy these earrings or those earrings?

Should I hire Ms. Carter or Mr. Price?

Should I buy a notebook computer or a desktop computer?

SIDE by SIDE JOURNAL

In your journal, compare your home town and the place you live now. Or compare any two places you know.

GRAMMAR FOCUS

COMPARATIVES

My new car is	faster larger bigger prettier	than my old car.
	more comfortable more attractive	

SHOULD

Should	I he she it we you they	study?

I He She It We You They	should study.

POSSESSIVE PRONOUNS

This dog is nicer than	mine. his. hers. ours. yours. theirs.

Complete the sentences.

1. A. Is your new computer fast?
   B. Yes. It's _____ than my old computer.

2. A. Is Jane's new neighborhood safe?
   B. Yes. It's _____ than her old neighborhood.

3. A. Is Livingston an interesting city?
   B. Yes. I think it's _____ than Centerville.

4. A. Is your new office big?
   B. Yes. It's _____ than my old office.

5. A. Is your new sofa comfortable?
   B. Yes. It's _____ than our old sofa.

6. A. Should my grandparents get a dog or a cat?
   B. They _____ get a dog. Dogs are very friendly. I think they're _____ than cats.

7. A. Should I order the chicken or the fish?
   B. I think you _____ order the fish. It's really good. It's _____ than the chicken.

Match the sentences.

___ 1. Is this your hat or your son's hat?
___ 2. Is this your pen or your wife's pen?
___ 3. Is this my jacket or your jacket?
___ 4. Is this your cat or your neighbors' cat?
___ 5. Is this Lucy's key or her brother's key?

a. It isn't yours. It's mine.
b. It isn't hers. It's his.
c. It isn't mine. It's hers.
d. It isn't mine. It's his.
e. It isn't ours. It's theirs.

1 CONVERSATION ASKING FOR ADVICE WHEN SHOPPING

Practice conversations with a classmate. Use the comparative form of any word in the box below to compare the items.

A. Which refrigerator do you recommend—this one or that one?

B. I recommend this one. It's larger than that one.

cheap	energy-efficient	large	quiet
comfortable	fast	new	reliable
easy-to-use	good	powerful	small

1. dishwasher

2. computer

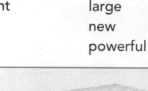
3. mattress

4. printer

5. cell phone

6. air conditioner

7. DVD player

8.

2 COMMUNITY CONNECTIONS STORES

Go to a department store or a discount store. Compare two different types of the same item. Which one do you recommend? Why is it better? Do this for five products. Write the information and share it with the class.

3 TEAMWORK ADVERTISEMENTS

Cut out some newspaper ads for the items on this page and other items. Bring the ads to class and work with a classmate. Compare two different types of each item. Which one is better? Why? Share your ads and opinions with the class.

Look at the advertisements. Choose the correct answer.

The 2011 Traveler
Larger, More Comfortable, & More Powerful than Last Year's Traveler!

- 7 inches longer — with two extra seats in the back.
- 1.5 inches higher means more headroom for taller drivers.
- 2 inches wider for more comfortable seating.
- New 330 horsepower engine — 50 pounds lighter and 10% more powerful than last year's engine.

From $30,000

Who Says that Bigger Is Better? Introducing the **Bantam**

Small on the Outside for Easy Parking

A Comfortable Interior that Feels Larger than It Is — with Seats for Five

You Won't Find a Safer, More Reliable Car at this Price!

From $18,000

"The Bantam is quieter and more comfortable than any other small car. With its efficient 120 horsepower engine, you won't have to worry about higher gas prices."
—ROAD & DRIVER MAGAZINE

1. There are _____ more seats in the 2011 Traveler than in the 2010 Traveler.
   A. two
   B. three
   C. four
   D. five

2. The 2011 Traveler has more headroom because it is _____.
   A. more powerful
   B. longer
   C. wider
   D. higher

3. The 2011 Traveler is _____ than the 2010 Traveler.
   A. one and a half inches longer
   B. two inches wider
   C. ten percent larger
   D. seven inches higher

4. According to the ad, the engine in the 2010 Traveler _____.
   A. was lighter than this year's engine
   B. wasn't as heavy as this year's engine
   C. wasn't as powerful as this year's engine
   D. wasn't as quiet as this year's engine

5. According to the second ad, _____.
   A. bigger is better
   B. the Bantam is difficult to park
   C. five people can ride in the Bantam
   D. the Bantam is safer and more reliable than any car at any price

6. According to *Road & Driver*, the Bantam _____.
   A. isn't as noisy as other small cars
   B. is more reliable than other small cars
   C. is higher than other small cars
   D. is more expensive than other small cars

7. The Bantam is probably a good car for people _____.
   A. who read magazines
   B. who drive in the city
   C. with very large families
   D. with a lot of money

8. In the second ad, *efficient* means _____.
   A. the engine is quiet
   B. the engine is powerful
   C. the engine is light
   D. the engine doesn't use much gas

Reading Tip

One of these questions is an **inference question**. The answer isn't a fact in the reading. You have to think about the information and decide what the best answer is. Which question on this page is an inference question? Which word in the question tells you that this is an inference question?

Read the letters to the editor and answer the questions.

To the Editor:

Students at Clarksdale High School took tests in English, math, history, and science last month, and their test scores were lower than ever before. As a high school parent, I can tell you why.

Classes at Clarksdale High are much larger than they should be, with more than forty students in a class. Teachers are using textbooks that are more than ten years old. There isn't any money for newer books. Finally, many good teachers are leaving Clarksdale to teach at other schools for higher pay.

It's time to spend more money on our high school. We might have to pay higher taxes, but our children are our future.

Marion Kane

To the Editor:

I'm writing in response to the article by James Alan Perry, *Clarksdale: A Better City for All*. In my opinion, after three years with Mayor Burns, Clarksdale is better for rich people, but not for the poor.

It's true that in the more expensive neighborhoods, the buses are newer and more reliable and the parks and streets are cleaner and safer. However, in the poorer sections of town, like East Clarksdale, the buses are never on time, and the streets and parks are dirtier and aren't as safe. Why aren't there more police officers in East Clarksdale? Why aren't the buses there as reliable as they are in other parts of town?

Ming Lee

To the Editor:

I grew up in Clarksdale and moved away ten years ago. Last month, I finally returned to visit and was very happy to see all the wonderful changes.

Clarksdale is a much more interesting town today than it was when I lived there. Main Street, with its attractive new restaurants, hotel, and movie theater, is a much more exciting place. I was also glad to see that there's a new bookstore downtown and that the library is in a bigger and more modern building.

Clarksdale isn't as quiet as it used to be, but that's okay with me. It's a more beautiful town with a lot more things to do.

Helen Sanders

1. According to Marion Kane, textbooks at the high school should be _____.
   A. bigger
   B. longer
   C. more difficult
   D. newer

2. According to Marion Kane, good teachers are leaving the high school because _____.
   A. their students' test scores are low
   B. they don't want to pay higher taxes
   C. they want more money for the work they do
   D. classes have more than 50 students

3. According to Ming Lee, East Clarksdale _____.
   A. has cleaner parks than other parts of town
   B. isn't as safe as other parts of town
   C. has newer buses than other parts of town
   D. has more police officers than other parts of town

4. According to Ming Lee, the buses in the more expensive neighborhoods of Clarksdale _____.
   A. are never on time
   B. aren't as reliable as they used to be
   C. are more reliable than they used to be
   D. aren't as reliable as the buses in East Clarksdale

5. Helen Sanders thinks Clarksdale _____ it used to be.
   A. isn't as beautiful as
   B. is noisier than
   C. isn't as interesting as
   D. isn't as attractive as

6. We can infer that Helen Sanders _____.
   A. likes to read
   B. lives near Clarksdale
   C. is a quiet person
   D. moved away to get a better job

WRITING Your Letter to the Editor Write a letter to the editor. Give your opinion about something you like or don't like about your city or town.

Choose the correct answer.

1. Our new living room furniture is very _____.
   A. intelligent
   B. comfortable
   C. honest
   D. friendly

2. It's important to eat _____ food.
   A. bad
   B. sympathetic
   C. large
   D. healthy

3. The subway system in our city is very _____.
   A. polite
   B. talkative
   C. reliable
   D. understanding

4. You shouldn't buy that coat. It isn't very _____.
   A. attractive
   B. spicy
   C. short
   D. neat

5. I think we should hire Ramon. He'll be a _____ secretary.
   A. lazy
   B. capable
   C. light
   D. wide

6. I like this watch. It's _____ than that one.
   A. busier
   B. more talented
   C. cheaper
   D. more hospitable

7. It's easy to park our new car because it's _____.
   A. large
   B. convenient
   C. comfortable
   D. small

8. My new car is faster than my old car. It has a _____ engine.
   A. more powerful
   B. wider
   C. higher
   D. longer

9. We're upset because students' test scores were _____ this year than last year.
   A. higher
   B. lower
   C. more difficult
   D. better

10. We need more police officers so our city will be _____.
   A. more sympathetic
   B. more useful
   C. safer
   D. newer

SKILLS CHECK ✔

Words:

☐ attractive	☐ dirty	☐ happy	☐ neat	☐ small
☐ beautiful	☐ easy	☐ healthy	☐ new	☐ smart
☐ big	☐ easy-to-use	☐ high	☐ nice	☐ snowy
☐ busy	☐ efficient	☐ honest	☐ polite	☐ soft
☐ capable	☐ energy-efficient	☐ hospitable	☐ poor	☐ spicy
☐ cheap	☐ exciting	☐ hot	☐ powerful	☐ sympathetic
☐ clean	☐ expensive	☐ intelligent	☐ pretty	☐ talented
☐ cold	☐ fancy	☐ interesting	☐ quiet	☐ talkative
☐ comfortable	☐ fashionable	☐ large	☐ rainy	☐ tall
☐ convenient	☐ fast	☐ lazy	☐ reliable	☐ understanding
☐ cool	☐ friendly	☐ light	☐ rich	☐ useful
☐ cute	☐ good – better	☐ long	☐ safe	☐ warm
☐ delicious	☐ handsome	☐ modern	☐ short	☐ wide

I can ask for advice:
☐ Should I *buy a dog or a cat*?
☐ Which *computer* do you recommend?

I can express my opinion:
☐ I think . . ./In my opinion, . . .
☐ I agree./I agree with you.
☐ I disagree./I disagree with you.

I can:
☐ compare items in a store
☐ compare items in advertisements

I can write:
☐ a comparison of places I know
☐ a letter to the editor

Superlatives

- Describing People, Places, and Things
- Shopping in a Department Store
- Expressing Opinions

- Store Directories
- Returning and Exchanging Items
- Using an ATM
- Checks
- Store Return Policies

VOCABULARY PREVIEW

1. energetic	6. lazy	11. patient
2. funny	7. mean	12. popular
3. generous	8. nice	13. rude
4. helpful	9. noisy	14. sloppy
5. honest	10. obnoxious	15. stubborn

49

The Smartest Person I Know

smart – the smartest	nice – the nicest
kind – the kindest	safe – the safest
funny – the funniest	big – the biggest
pretty – the prettiest	hot – the hottest

A. I think your friend Margaret is very **smart**.

B. She certainly is. She's **the smartest** person I know.

1. *your Aunt Emma*
kind

2. *your friend Jim*
bright

3. *your parents*
nice

4. *your Uncle Ted*
funny

5. *your sister*
pretty

6. *your cousin Amy*
friendly

7. *Larry*
lazy

8. *your landlord*
mean

9. *your roommates*
sloppy

The Most Energetic Person I Know

smart – the smartest	energetic – the most energetic
funny – the funniest	interesting – the most interesting
nice – the nicest	patient – the most patient
big – the biggest	stubborn – the most stubborn

A. I think your grandmother is very **energetic**.

B. She certainly is. She's **the most energetic** person I know.

1. *your friend Carlos interesting*

2. *your grandfather generous*

3. *your cousins talented*

4. *our English teacher patient*

5. *your nephew Andrew stubborn*

6. *your younger brother polite*

7. *your older sister bright*

8. *your upstairs neighbor noisy*

9. *your downstairs neighbor rude*

10. *Senator Smith honest*

11. *our history professor boring*

12.

THE NICEST PERSON

friendly · polite · smart · talented · pretty

Mr. and Mrs. Jackson are very proud of their daughter, Linda. She's a very nice person. She's friendly, she's polite, she's smart, and she's talented. She's also very pretty.

Mr. and Mrs. Jackson's friends and neighbors always compliment them about Linda. They say she's the nicest person they know. According to them, she's the friendliest, the most polite, the smartest, and the most talented girl in the neighborhood. They also think she's the prettiest.

Mr. and Mrs. Jackson agree. They think Linda is a wonderful girl, and they're proud to say she's their daughter.

THE MOST OBNOXIOUS DOG

noisy · stubborn · lazy · mean · ugly

Mr. and Mrs. Hubbard are very embarrassed by their dog, Rex. He's a very obnoxious dog. He's noisy, he's stubborn, he's lazy, and he's mean. He's also very ugly.

Mr. and Mrs. Hubbard's friends and neighbors always complain about Rex. They say he's the most obnoxious dog they know. According to them, he's the noisiest, the most stubborn, the laziest, and the meanest dog in the neighborhood. They also think he's the ugliest.

Mr. and Mrs. Hubbard agree. They think Rex is a horrible dog, and they're ashamed to say he's theirs.

✓ READING *CHECK-UP*

CHOOSE

1. Linda is the (most polite   smart) person I know.
2. She's the most (talented   friendliest) girl in the neighborhood.
3. She's a very (nicest   nice) person.
4. Rex is the most (stubborn   mean) dog in the neighborhood.
5. He's the (lazy   noisiest) dog I know.
6. He's also the most (ugliest   obnoxious) dog in town.

Q & A

The neighbors are talking. Using these models, create dialogs based on the stories.

A. You know . . . I think Linda is very *nice*.
B. I agree. She's the *nicest* girl in the neighborhood.

A. You know . . . I think Rex is very *obnoxious*.
B. You're right. He's the *most obnoxious* dog in the neighborhood.

How About You?

Tell about the nicest person you know.

How to Say It!

Expressing an Opinion

A. { In my opinion, . . .
As far as I'm concerned, . . .
If you ask me, . . . } Linda is the most talented student in our school.

B. I agree. / I disagree.

Practice conversations with other students. Share opinions.

LISTENING

Listen to the sentence. Is the person saying something good or something bad about someone else?

1. a. good   b. bad
2. a. good   b. bad
3. a. good   b. bad
4. a. good   b. bad
5. a. good   b. bad
6. a. good   b. bad
7. a. good   b. bad
8. a. good   b. bad
9. a. good   b. bad

PRONUNCIATION *Linking Words with Duplicated Consonants*

Listen. Then say it.

She's the nicest teacher in our school.

He's the most stubborn neighbor on our street.

They're the most talented dancers in the world.

Say it. Then listen.

He's the most generous student in our class.

This is the cheapest toothpaste in the store.

He's the most polite taxi driver in the city.

53

I Want to Buy a Small Radio

a small radio
a smaller radio
the smallest radio

a comfortable chair
a more comfortable chair
the most comfortable chair

a good car
a better car
the best car

A. May I help you?

B. Yes, please. I want to buy a **small** radio.

A. I think you'll like this one. It's VERY **small**.

B. Don't you have a **smaller** one?

A. No, I'm afraid not. This is **the smallest** one we have.

B. Thank you anyway.

A. Sorry we can't help you. Please come again.

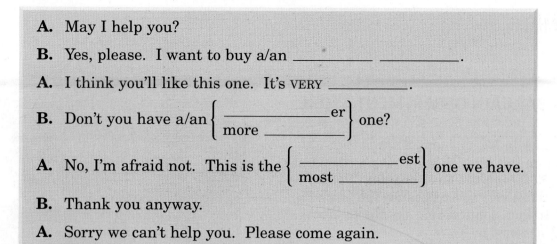

A. May I help you?

B. Yes, please. I want to buy a/an _____ _____.

A. I think you'll like this one. It's VERY _____.

B. Don't you have a/an { _____er / more _____ } one?

A. No, I'm afraid not. This is the { _____est / most _____ } one we have.

B. Thank you anyway.

A. Sorry we can't help you. Please come again.

1. *large TV*

2. *comfortable rocking chair*

3. *good CD player*

4. *cheap watch*

5. *fast printer*

6. *elegant evening gown*

7. *small cell phone*

8. *lightweight video camera*

9. *powerful computer*

10. *tall bookcase*

11. *short novel*

12.

BOB'S BARGAIN DEPARTMENT STORE

Bob's Bargain Department Store is the cheapest store in town. However, even though it's the cheapest, it isn't the most popular. People don't shop there very often because the products are bad.* In fact, some people say the products there are the worst in town.

The furniture isn't very comfortable, the clothes aren't very fashionable, the appliances aren't very dependable, and the home entertainment products aren't very good. Besides that, the location isn't very convenient, and the salespeople aren't very helpful.

That's why people don't shop at Bob's Bargain Department Store very often, even though it's the cheapest store in town.

THE LORD AND LADY DEPARTMENT STORE

The Lord and Lady Department Store sells very good products. In fact, some people say the products there are the best in town.

They sell the most comfortable furniture, the most fashionable clothes, the most dependable appliances, and the best home entertainment products. And besides that, their location is the most convenient, and their salespeople are the most helpful in town.

However, even though the Lord and Lady Department Store is the best store in town, people don't shop there very often because it's also the most expensive.

* bad – worse – worst

THE SUPER SAVER DEPARTMENT STORE

The Super Saver Department Store is the most popular store in town. It isn't the cheapest, and it isn't the most expensive. It doesn't have the best products, and it doesn't have the worst.

The furniture isn't the most comfortable you can buy, but it's more comfortable than the furniture at many other stores. The clothes aren't the most fashionable you can buy, but they're more fashionable than the clothes at many other stores. The appliances aren't the most dependable you can buy, but they're more dependable than the appliances at many other stores. The home entertainment products aren't the best you can buy, but they're better than the home entertainment products at many other stores. In addition, the location is convenient, and the salespeople are helpful.

You can see why the Super Saver Department Store is the most popular store in town. The prices are reasonable, and the products are good. That's why people like to shop there.

 **READING** *CHECK-UP*

TRUE OR FALSE?

1. Bob's Bargain Department Store is the most popular store in town.
2. The salespeople at Lord and Lady are more helpful than the salespeople at Super Saver.
3. The location of Lord and Lady isn't as convenient as the location of Bob's.
4. The Super Saver Department Store has the best prices in town.
5. The home entertainment products at Super Saver are better than the home entertainment products at Bob's.
6. People in this town say the cheapest department store is the best.

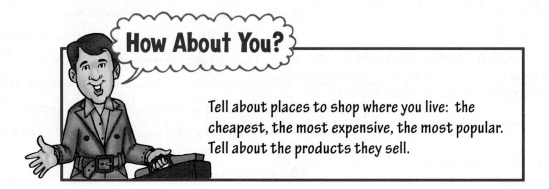

How About You?

Tell about places to shop where you live: the cheapest, the most expensive, the most popular. Tell about the products they sell.

INTERACTIONS *Sharing Opinions*

Practice conversations with other students. Share opinions, and give reasons for your opinions.

In your opinion, . . .

1. Who is the most popular actor/actress in your country? Who is the most popular TV star? the best singer?

2. What is the most popular car in your country? the most popular sport? the best newspaper? the most popular magazine? the best TV program? the most popular food?

3. What is the best city in your country? What is the worst city? Why? What are the most interesting tourist sights in your country? What are the most popular vacation places?

4. Who is the most important person in your country now? Why? Who was the most important person in the history of your country? Why?

SIDE by SIDE JOURNAL

Who is the most important person in your life? Why? Write about this person in your journal.

GRAMMAR FOCUS

SUPERLATIVES

| He's | the smartest
the nicest
the biggest
the busiest | person I know. |
| | the most talented
the most interesting | |

Complete the sentences.

1. A. I'm looking for a fast computer.
   B. This is _____ computer we sell.

2. A. Your sister Susan is very intelligent.
   B. I agree. She's _____ person I know.

3. A. I'm looking for a big refrigerator.
   B. This is _____ refrigerator in the store.

4. A. Our cousins are very nice.
   B. I agree. They're _____ people in our family.

5. A. Is this camera lightweight?
   B. Yes. It's _____ camera you can find.

6. A. Our history teacher is very interesting.
   B. I agree. I think he's _____ teacher in the school.

7. A. This dress is very fashionable.
   B. I think it's _____ dress in the store.

8. A. I'm looking for a good DVD player.
   B. This is _____ one we sell.

9. A. Are your upstairs neighbors friendly?
   B. Yes. They're _____ people in our building.

10. A. Are the products at that store bad?
    B. Yes. I think they're _____ products in town.

58

1 CONVERSATION   LOCATING ITEMS IN A DEPARTMENT STORE

STORE DIRECTORY

DEPARTMENT	FLOOR
Children's Clothing Women's Clothing	1
Men's Clothing	2
Electronics Housewares	3
Furniture Household Appliances	4

Practice conversations with a classmate. Use the directory to find the correct department and floor for these items and others.

A. Excuse me. Where can I find refrigerators?
B. In the Household Appliances department on the fourth floor.
A. Thank you.

1.   2.    3.   4.   5.

2 CONVERSATION   RETURNING & EXCHANGING ITEMS

Practice conversations with a classmate.

A. I'd like to return this/these _____.
B. What's the matter with it/them?
A. It's/They're too _____.
B. Would you like to exchange it/them?
A. No, thank you. I'd like a refund, please.
B. Do you have your receipt?
A. Yes. Here it is.

1. sweater   2. jeans   3. pants   4. dress   5.
   tight   large   long   short

3 TEAMWORK   CATEGORIZING

Bring department store ads to class. Work with a classmate. On a piece of paper, write the names of the store departments on this page. Then list items in your ads in the correct department.

USING AN ATM

Look at the ATM screens and answer the questions.

WELCOME TO
FIRST BANK
24 HOUR ATM

INSERT YOUR CARD

Enter your PIN on the keypad.

****

Then press OKAY.

OKAY

Select a Transaction.

TRANSFERS   FAST CASH $60 from Checking

BALANCE INQUIRY   WITHDRAWAL

DEPOSIT   DEPOSIT with CASH BACK

1. *Insert your card* means ____.
   A. take your card
   B. put your card in the machine
   C. use your card
   D. return your card

2. Your PIN is your ____.
   A. social security number
   B. bank account number
   C. telephone number
   D. personal identification number

3. After you enter your PIN, you ____.
   A. enter the bank
   B. insert your ATM card
   C. select a transaction
   D. deposit money

4. To put $100 in your checking account, select ____.
   A. Deposit
   B. Balance Inquiry
   C. Fast Cash
   D. Withdrawal

5. To find out how much money is in your account, select ____.
   A. Transfers
   B. Balance Inquiry
   C. Deposit with Cash Back
   D. Withdrawal

6. To move money from one account to another, select ____.
   A. Fast Cash
   B. Balance Inquiry
   C. Transfers
   D. Deposit with Cash Back

READING CHECKS

Look at the check. Decide if the following sentences are True (T) or False (F).

Mario Gomez
Susan Gomez

105

Date April 9, 2011

Pay to the order of Northern Electric Company $ 56.34

Fifty-six and 34/100 ———— Dollars

Camden Savings Bank

For electric bill 2/15-3/15 account #146056   Mario Gomez

⑆3111040178⑆139057813⑈105⑈

____ 1. Northern Electric Company wrote this check on April 9, 2011.

____ 2. The check is for fifty-six dollars and thirty-four cents.

____ 3. Mario Gomez is paying the electric bill.

____ 4. The bill is for the month of April.

____ 5. Susan Gomez can also write checks with this checking account.

____ 6. 146056 is the checking account number.

Read this sign in a Customer Service Department and answer the questions.

Gray's
Department Store   *Our Return Policy*

- We are happy to accept returns on most items within 90 days of the date of purchase.
- Exceptions to our 90-day return policy:
  - We will accept returns within 45 days of the date of purchase on computers, monitors, printers, and other computer components.
  - We will accept returns within 30 days of the date of purchase on CDs, DVDs, and computer software **ONLY** if they are unopened.
  - We will **NOT** accept returns on holiday items after the date of the holiday.
  - We will **NOT** accept returns on underwear, swimsuits, or items marked *Final Sale*.
- When you return items with a receipt, you can exchange the item or receive a refund. Your refund depends on your method of payment:

Method of Payment	Refund
Cash or debit card	Cash refund
Check (within the last 10 days)	Store credit
Check (more than 10 days ago)	Cash refund
Credit card	Credit to your account
Store credit card or gift card	Store credit

- Without a receipt, you can exchange the item for the same item in a different size or color, or you can receive a store credit for the lowest sale price of that item within the last 90 days. You need to present a photo I.D. at the time of the return. Gray's Department Store does not have to accept your return when there is no receipt.
- You can return items at any Gray's Department Store in the United States or Canada. The original price tag should be attached to the item.
- You can return defective items—items that are broken, ripped, or unsafe—at any time with or without a receipt. We will exchange or repair the defective item.

1. You have to return a computer monitor _____.
   A. within 30 days
   B. within 45 days
   C. within 90 days
   D. to the store where you bought it

2. You can return _____ 89 days after you buy it.
   A. a jacket
   B. a CD
   C. a swimsuit
   D. a printer

3. You CANNOT return _____.
   A. defective items
   B. unopened DVDs
   C. items marked *Final Sale*
   D. items with a price tag attached

4. You can receive a cash refund when you pay with _____.
   A. a credit card
   B. a check that is five days old
   C. a gift card
   D. a check that is eleven days old

5. When you don't have a receipt, _____.
   A. you have to show a photo I.D.
   B. you can't return the item
   C. you might receive a cash refund
   D. you can't exchange the item

6. You can return _____.
   A. a CD that you bought 2 months ago
   B. a computer that doesn't work
   C. computer software in an opened box
   D. a Christmas tree on January tenth

Choose the correct answer.

1. Everybody compliments us about our son. They say he's the _____ boy in the neighborhood.
   A. worst
   B. laziest
   C. friendliest
   D. most boring

2. The new shopping mall is in a very _____ location.
   A. short
   B. convenient
   C. lightweight
   D. energetic

3. George is a wonderful salesperson. He's always _____.
   A. helpful
   B. noisy
   C. rude
   D. sloppy

4. Our store sells the most _____ appliances in the city.
   A. patient
   B. generous
   C. honest
   D. dependable

5. Nobody in our building likes the man in Apartment 5. He's very _____.
   A. popular
   B. nice
   C. mean
   D. kind

6. My niece always says, "Thank you" and "You're welcome." She's the most _____ little girl I know.
   A. stubborn
   B. polite
   C. horrible
   D. obnoxious

7. To use the ATM, insert your _____ and enter your PIN.
   A. key
   B. money
   C. account
   D. card

8. I'm going to _____ money from my savings account to my checking account.
   A. transfer
   B. balance
   C. use
   D. select

9. I need to return this video camera to the store because _____.
   A. it was marked *Final Sale*
   B. it has the original price tag
   C. it's defective
   D. I paid with a credit card

10. Excuse me. Can you help me? I'd like to _____ this sports jacket for a larger size.
    A. accept
    B. exchange
    C. attach
    D. receive

SKILLS CHECK ✔

Words:
□ bad–worse–worst
□ boring
□ bright
□ cheap
□ comfortable
□ convenient
□ dependable
□ elegant
□ energetic
□ fashionable
□ fast
□ friendly
□ funny
□ generous
□ good–better–best
□ helpful
□ honest
□ horrible
□ interesting
□ kind
□ large
□ lazy
□ lightweight
□ long
□ mean
□ nice
□ noisy
□ obnoxious
□ patient
□ polite
□ popular
□ powerful
□ pretty
□ rude
□ short
□ sloppy
□ small
□ smart
□ stubborn
□ talented
□ ugly
□ wonderful
□ deposit
□ enter
□ insert
□ press
□ balance
□ card
□ cash
□ checking
□ key
□ PIN
□ savings
□ transfer
□ withdrawal
□ exchange
□ return
□ credit card
□ debit card
□ date of purchase
□ defective
□ final sale
□ gift card
□ price tag
□ receipt
□ refund
□ store credit

I can ask & answer:
□ May I help you? Yes, please. I want to buy *a small radio*.
□ Where can I find *refrigerators*?
□ I'd like to return this/these _____. What's the matter with it/them?

I can read:
□ a department store directory
□ ATM screens
□ checks
□ a department store return policy

I can write about:
□ the most important person in my life

Did You Know?

The longest car in the world is 100 feet long. It has 26 wheels, a swimming pool, and a waterbed!

The world's biggest costume party is the Carnival celebration in Brazil. Every day during Carnival, more than 50,000 people walk through the streets in costumes.

The largest subway station in the world is Grand Central Terminal in New York City. Every day more than half a million people pass through the station.

The biggest igloo in the world is the Ice Hotel in Sweden. It has rooms for 150 guests. Every year workers have to rebuild the hotel because it melts in the spring!

FACT FILE

World Geography Facts

- The longest river in the world is the Nile. It is 4,180 miles (6,690 kilometers) long.

- The highest mountain in the world is Mount Everest. It is 29,028 feet (8,848 meters) high.

- The largest ocean in the world is the Pacific Ocean. It is 64,000,000 square miles (165,760,000 square kilometers).

- The biggest desert in the world is the Sahara. It is 3,500,270 square miles (9,065,000 square kilometers).

BUILD YOUR VOCABULARY!

Adjectives with Negative Prefixes

They're _____ .

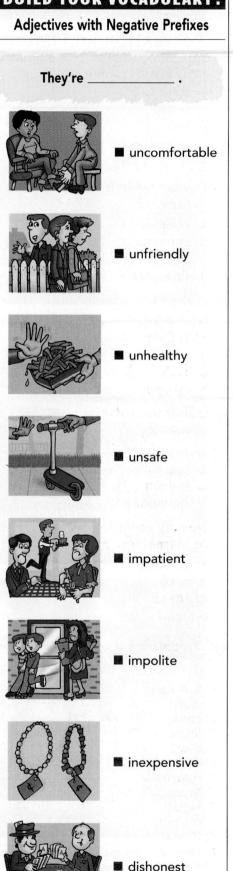

- uncomfortable
- unfriendly
- unhealthy
- unsafe
- impatient
- impolite
- inexpensive
- dishonest

AROUND THE WORLD

Recreation and Entertainment

The most popular type of outdoor recreation in France is camping. Every night 3 million people in France sleep outside.

Movies are the most popular type of entertainment in India. Every day 15 million people in India go to the movies.

The most popular sport in the world is football. This game is called "soccer" in the United States. More than 100,000,000 people play football in over 150 countries.

What are the most popular types of recreation and entertainment in different countries you know?

Global Exchange

IvanaG: I'm going on vacation with my family tomorrow. We're going to the most popular beach in our country. We'll stay there for a week in a small hotel. It isn't the best hotel there, but it's the friendliest and the closest to the beach. We go there every year. It's a lot of fun! The water is clear, and the air is fresh. My sister and my brother and I swim all day, and we go to an amusement park in the evening. I think it has the largest roller-coaster in the world! So I'll write again when I get back and tell you all about our vacation.

P.S. Do you have a favorite vacation place? Where is it? When do you go there? What do you do?

Send a message to a keypal. Tell about a favorite vacation place in your country.

LISTENING

And Now a Word From Our Sponsors!

b **1** Rings & Things   **a.** furniture

____ **2** Big Value Store   **b.** jewelry

____ **3** Comfort Kingdom   **c.** sports equipment

____ **4** Electric City   **d.** appliances

____ **5** Recreation Station   **e.** home entertainment products

What Are They Saying?

The biggest! The smallest! The fastest! The most exciting!

APPENDIX

Listening Scripts

Unit 1 – Page 9

Listen and choose the correct answer.

1. What are you going to do tomorrow?
2. What do you do in the summer?
3. When did you clean your apartment?
4. What did you give your parents for their anniversary?
5. Where did you and your friends go yesterday?
6. How often do they send messages to each other?
7. What did he give her?
8. When are you going to make pancakes?

Unit 2 – Page 16

Listen and choose what the people are talking about.

1. A. How much do you want?
   B. Just a little, please.
2. A. Do you want some more?
   B. Okay. But just a few.
3. A. These are delicious!
   B. I'm glad you like them.
4. A. I ate too many.
   B. How many did you eat?
5. A. They're bad for my health.
   B. Really?
6. A. It's very good.
   B. Thank you.
7. A. Would you care for some more?
   B. Yes, but not too much.
8. A. There isn't any.
   B. There isn't?!

Unit 3 – Page 22

Listen and choose what the people are talking about.

1. A. How much does a gallon cost?
   B. Two seventy-nine.
2. A. They're very expensive this week.
   B. You're right.
3. A. How many loaves do we need?
   B. Three.
4. A. Sorry. There aren't any more.
   B. There aren't?!
5. A. I need two pounds.
   B. Two pounds? Okay.
6. A. How much does the large box cost?
   B. Five thirty-nine.
7. A. How many cans do we need?
   B. Three.
8. A. I bought too much.
   B. Really?

Side by Side Gazette – Page 28

Listen and match the products and the prices.

1. Attention, food shoppers! Thank you for shopping at Save-Rite Supermarket! Crispy Cereal is on sale this week. A box of Crispy Cereal is only three dollars and forty-nine cents. Three forty-nine is a very good price for Crispy Cereal. So buy some today!
2. Attention, shoppers! Right now in the bakery section whole wheat bread is on sale. Buy a loaf of whole wheat bread for only two seventy-five. That's right! Just two seventy-five! The bread is hot and fresh. So come to the bakery section and get a loaf now!
3. Thank you for shopping at Sunny Supermarket! We have a special low price on orange juice today. A quart of orange juice is only a dollar seventy-nine. Orange juice is in Aisle 5, next to the milk.
4. Hello, food shoppers! It's 95 degrees today. It's a good day for Sorelli's ice cream! Sorelli's ice cream comes in vanilla, chocolate, and other delicious flavors. And today, a pint of Sorelli's ice cream is only three twenty-five!
5. Welcome to Bartley's Supermarket! We have a special today on bananas. You can buy bananas for only forty cents a pound. Bananas are good for you! So walk over to our fruit section and buy a bunch of bananas today!

Unit 4 – Page 37

WHAT'S THE LINE?

Mrs. Harris (from the story on page 36) is calling Tommy and Julie's school. Listen and choose the correct lines.

1. Good morning. Park Elementary School.
2. Yes, Mrs. Harris. What can I do for you?
3. Oh? What's the matter?
4. That's too bad. Are you going to take them to the doctor?
5. Well, I hope Tommy and Julie feel better soon.

WHAT'S THE WORD?

Listen and choose the word you hear.

1. I might go to school tomorrow.
2. I want to come to work today.
3. Don't walk there!
4. We'll be ready in half an hour.
5. They'll go to school tomorrow.
6. Don't stand there! You might get hit!
7. I call the doctor when I'm sick.
8. Watch your step! There are wet spots on the floor.
9. I'm sick and tired of sailing.

Unit 5 – Page 44

Listen and choose what the people are talking about.

1. A. I like it. It's fast.
   B. It is. It's much faster than my old one.
2. A. Is it comfortable?
   B. Yes. It's more comfortable than my old one.
3. A. I think it should be shorter.
   B. But it's very short now!
4. A. They aren't very polite.
   B. You're right. They should be more polite.
5. A. Is it safe?
   B. Yes. It's much safer than my old one.
6. A. Which one should I buy?
   B. Buy this one. It's more powerful than that one.

Unit 6 – Page 53

Listen to the sentence. Is the person saying something good or something bad about someone else?

1. She's the nicest person I know.
2. He's the laziest student in our class.
3. He's the most boring person I know.
4. She's the most generous person in our family.
5. They're the most honest people I know.
6. He's the rudest person in our apartment building.
7. He's the most dependable person in our office.
8. She's the kindest neighbor on our street.
9. She's the most stubborn person I know.

Side by Side Gazette – Page 60

Listen and match the products.

ANNOUNCER: Are you looking for a special gift for a special person in your life? A birthday gift? An anniversary present? Come to Rings & Things—the best store in town for rings, necklaces, earrings, bracelets, and other fine things. Rings & Things— on Main Street downtown, or at the East Side Mall.

FRIEND 1: That was an excellent dinner!
FRIEND 2: Thank you. I'm glad you liked it.
FRIEND 1: Can I help you wash the dishes?
FRIEND 2: Thanks. But they're already in the dishwasher.
FRIEND 1: Is your dishwasher on?
FRIEND 2: Yes, it is.
FRIEND 1: I can't believe it! Your dishwasher is MUCH quieter than mine.
FRIEND 2: It's new. We got it at the Big Value Store. They sell the quietest dishwashers in town.
ANNOUNCER: That's right. The Big Value Store sells the quietest dishwashers in town. We also have the largest refrigerators, the most powerful washing machines, and the best ovens. And we also have the best prices! So come to the Big Value Store, on Airport Road, open seven days a week.

PERSON WHO CAN'T FALL ASLEEP: Oh, I can't believe it! It's three o'clock in the morning, and I can't fall asleep.

This bed is so uncomfortable! I need a new bed. I need a new bed NOW!

ANNOUNCER: Do you have this problem? Is your bed uncomfortable? Come to Comfort Kingdom for the most comfortable beds you can buy. We also have the most beautiful sofas and the most attractive tables and chairs in the city. And our salespeople are the friendliest and the most helpful in town. So visit Comfort Kingdom today because life is short, and you should be comfortable!

ANNOUNCER: I'm standing here today in front of Electric City so we can talk to a typical customer. Here's a typical customer now. He's leaving the store with a large box. Let's ask him a question. Excuse me, sir. May I ask you a question?
CUSTOMER: Certainly.
ANNOUNCER: What did you buy today?
CUSTOMER: A VCR.
ANNOUNCER: And why did you buy it at Electric City?
CUSTOMER: Because Electric City has the cheapest and the most dependable products in town.
ANNOUNCER: Is this your first time at Electric City?
CUSTOMER: Oh, no! Last year I bought a radio here, and the year before I bought a TV.
ANNOUNCER: And are you happy with those products?
CUSTOMER: Absolutely! The radio is much better than my old one, and the picture on my TV is much bigger and brighter.
ANNOUNCER: So are you a happy customer?
CUSTOMER: Definitely! There's no place like Electric City. It's the best store in town.
ANNOUNCER: Well, there you have it! Another happy Electric City customer. Visit an Electric City store near YOU today!

ANNOUNCER: This is it! It's the biggest sale of the year, and it's this weekend at Recreation Station! That's right. Everything is on sale—sneakers, tennis rackets, footballs, basketballs—everything in the store! It's all on sale at Recreation Station. We're the largest! We're the most convenient! We're the best! And this weekend we're the cheapest! It's the biggest sale of the year, and it's this weekend— only at Recreation Station!

Vocabulary List

Numbers indicate the pages on which the words first appear.

Actions and Activities

accept 58c
add 24
agree 47
apply 10c
arrive 29
ask 53
attend 10c
bake 13
become 32
begin 10c
believe 16
bloom 32
buy 8
call 9
call in sick 36
celebrate 10b
change (v) 46
chat online 2
chop up 24
clean 5
come 18c
come home 44
communicate 8
complain 52
compliment 52
connect 18c
continue 10c
cook 3
cost 21
cut 24
decide 23
deliver 27
depend 38c
deposit (v) 58b
disagree 47
do 5
drink 23
drive 4
drown 35
eat 2
end 29
enjoy 25
enter 10c
exchange 58c
fall (v) 34
fall asleep 35

feel 36
finish 10c
fire (v) 43
follow 10c
forget 7
get back 60
get home 22
get married 29
get out of 30
get to 33
give 6
give advice 8
go 8
go out 42
go outside 32
go to bed 22
go to school 36
go to work 36
graduate 10c
grow up 8
have 13
help (v) 8
hire 43
hope 36
hurry 32
hurt 34
insert 58b
invite 38c
keep 27
keep refrigerated 26b
know 6
leave 10c
lend 8
like 2
listen 9
live 8
look 22
lose 8
make 12
make a list 12
make *pancakes* 4
marry 38
melt 59
miss 46
mix in 24
move 8
move away 48c
name 29
need 18c

offer 38c
open (v) 22
order (v) 25
paint (v) 32
pass through 59
pay 10c
plan 38c
plant (v) 4
pour in 24
prepare 10c
present (v) 58c
press 58b
produce (v) 27
put 24
put on 34
read 2
rebuild 59
receive 58c
recommend 23
register 10a
rent (v) 43
repeat 34
request 38b
return 29
ride 32
RSVP 38b
rush 22
say 9
see 31
seem 44
select 58b
sell 8
send 8
serve 38c
set up 18c
shop 27
show 38c
sit down 22
skate 5
ski 5
slice (v) 24
spend 16
stand 34
start 10c
stay 38c
stay home 36
stay indoors 32
step on 35
study 10c

suggest 23
take 8
take piano lessons 43
talk 9
taste 17
teach 10c
tell 17
think 6
touch 34
transfer 58b
try 44
turn on 18c
use 18c
visit 44
vote 42
wait 31
walk out 16
want 14
watch (v) 34
watch TV 2
watch videos 4
wear 44
wonder 16
work 30
worry 35
write 3

Ailments, Symptoms, and Injuries

break *my* leg 35
cold 32
fall 34
flu 36
get a shock 34
get hit 34
get hurt 34
hurt *your* eyes 34
hurt *your* head 34
measles 36
nauseous 36
seasick 35
sick 35
spots 36
sunburn 35

Animals, Birds, and Insects

cat 37
dog 40

plug 18c
polka dots 7
present 6
product 56
radio 54
recipe 24
roller coaster 35
saucepan 24
shopping list 20
story 32
table 18c
thing 60
ton 25
toothpaste 53
tree 32
TV 2
video 4
video camera 55
water 60
wig 40
wire 34

Occupations

actor 58
actress 58
attorney-at-law 58c
chef 10b
dancer 53
doctor 10c
landlord 50
mayor 46
police officer 48c
professor 43
senator 51
singer 58
teacher 24
TV star 58
waiter 25
waitress 25

Parts of the Body

arm 36
eyes 34
feet 35
hair 44
hand 43
head 34
leg 35

People

boss 45
boy 32
children 10b
girl 52

guest 30
neighbor 52
people 10b
person 50
salespeople 56
student 10c
teenager 44
worker 59

Personal Information 10a

address
age
apartment
city
date of birth
first name
last name
name
state
street
zip code

Places in the Community

amusement park 60
bakery 28
beach 2
book store 48c
church 8
city 47
college 8
day-care center 10c
department store 56
food store 27
grocery store 27
high school 8
hospital 8
hotel 48c
mall 2
movie theater 48c
neighborhood 31
open market 27
park 32
place 27
restaurant 25
school 33
station 59
subway 59
subway station 59
supermarket 16
tourist sight 58
town 56

university 10c
wholesale store 27

Recreation Activities

dance 5
go dancing 35
go hiking 2
go sailing 35
go skating 10b
go skiing 5
go swimming 35
go to the movies 35
play (v) 3
play baseball 32
play basketball 2
play tennis 9
play the piano 3
swim 3
take a vacation 8
take a walk 35

School/Education

auditorium 18a
cafeteria 18a
cafeteria worker 18a
community college 10c
computer lab 18b
course 43
education 10c
elementary school 10c
grade 10c
grades 44
graduate school 10c
guidance counselor 18a
guidance office 18a
gym 18a
hall 18a
high school 8
high school student 10b
history professor 51
homework 10b
kindergarten 10c
librarian 18a
library 18a
math 48c
middle school 10c
music teacher 18a
nurse's office 18a
P.E. teacher 18a
pre-school 10c
principal 18a
principal's office 18a

private school 10c
public school 10c
public school education 10c
school 10a
school nurse 18a
school office 18b
school registration form 10a
school secretary 18a
science 48c
science lab 18a
security officer 18a
student 10c
technical school 10c
test 31
test score 48c
textbook 48c
university 10c
vocational school 10c

Seasons 1

spring
summer
fall/autumn
winter

Sports and Recreation

camping 60
football 60
fun 60
game 30
recreation 60
soccer 60
sport 58
sports equipment 60
swimming pool 59
tennis racket 40
walk 32

Telephone

cell phone 40

Time Expressions

a minute 24
all the time 17
all *year* 32
at *7:00* 30
day 1
early in the *evening* 28
evening 25
every day 3
every *morning* 36

for *45* minutes **24**
for a long time **27**
for many *years* **8**
for *three* hours **24**
hour **24**
in a few hours **30**
in a few minutes **30**
in a few more *weeks* **32**
in a little while **30**
in a week **30**
in an hour **30**
in *five* minutes **30**
in half an hour **30**
in the past **27**
in *two* or *three* days **30**
last January/February/
.../December **4**
last night **4**
last spring/summer/fall
(autumn)/winter **4**
last Sunday/Monday/
.../Saturday **4**
last week/weekend/
month/year **4**

month **1**
next *Saturday* **33**
now **8**
on *Sunday* afternoons
32
on time **38c**
on the weekend **2**
once or twice a week
27
right after **38c**
right away **38c**
right now **3**
season **1**
some day **31**
the middle of the
afternoon **28**
these days **27**
this January/February/
.../December **5**
this morning/afternoon/
evening **4**
this spring/summer/fall
(autumn)/winter **4**
this Sunday/Monday/
.../Saturday **5**

this week/weekend/
month/year **4**
time **27**
today **4**
tomorrow **3**
tomorrow morning/
afternoon/evening/
night **9**
tonight **5**
two years ago **6**
week **27**
weekend **2**
year **1**
yesterday **3**
yesterday morning/
afternoon/evening **4**

Transportation

bus system **46**
car **42**
motorcycle **42**
sports car **40**
train **30**
van **8**
wheel **59**

Weather

cold **47**
cool **47**
hot **47**
rain (v) **31**
rainy **47**
snow (n) **32**
snowy **47**
sunny **32**
warm **32**
weather **31**

Work

boss **45**
company **27**
company picnic **35**
helmet **29**
job **8**
machine **34**
office **36**
safety glasses **29**
skills **10c**
work **22**
worker **59**

Skill Index

BASIC LANGUAGE SKILLS

Listening, 9, 16, 22, 28, 37, 44, 53, 60

Pronunciation, 9, 18, 26, 37, 48, 53

Speaking
(*Throughout*)

Reading/Document literacy
Abbreviations:
  Days of the week, 1
  Months of the year, 1
  Weights and measurements, 20
Advertisements, 48b
ATM instructions, 58b
Articles/Academic reading, 10c, 27, 38c
Calendar, 1, 10b
Charts, 58c
Checks, 58b
Diagram, 18b, 18c
Email, 28, 60
Facts, 27, 59
Floor plan, 18b
Food labels, 26b
Instructions for a procedure, 18c
Invitations, 38b
Letters to the editor, 48c
Menu, 26c
Newspaper, finding information in, 48a, 58a
Recipe, 24
Shopping list, 20
Store directory, 26a, 58a
Store policies, 58c
Store receipt, 26b, 26d

Stories, short structured, 8, 16, 17, 22, 25, 32, 36, 44, 46, 52, 56, 57
Strategies, reading:
  Facts and inferences, 18b
  Inference questions, 48b
  Signal words, 38c

Writing
Addresses, 10a
Charts, writing information in, 18a
Checks, 58b
Compositions, 9
Dates, 10a
Email, 28, 60
Forms, filling out, 10a
Invitations, 38b
Journal writing, 7, 18, 26, 37, 48, 58
Letter to the editor, 48c
Lists, 12, 20
Names, 10a, 18a
Note to a teacher explaining a child's absence, 37
Recipe, 24
Shopping list, 20
Telephone numbers, 10a

NUMBERS/NUMERACY/MATH

(The Numbers Worksheets in the Side by Side Plus *Multilevel Activity & Achievement Test Book & CD-ROM provide practice with numbers and math for each unit.)*
Address numbers, 10a
Advertisements, numbers in, 48b
Cardinal numbers, 26a
Checks, 58b
Dates, 7, 10a, 38b

Elapsed time, 58c
Food labels, 26b
Money, amounts of, 21, 28
Ordinal numbers, 7, 10a–b, 58a
Percents, 26b
Prices, 21, 26b–d
Quantity, indicating, 20
Receipts, 26b, 26d
Room numbers, 18b
Statistical information, 27, 59
Store directories, numbers in, 26a, 58a
Time, 38b

LEARNING SKILLS
Academic concepts:
  Cross-cultural expectations, 38c
  Education system, American, 10c
  Food shopping, 27
  Statistical information, 27, 59
Categorization, 26a, 58a
Charts, information, 58c
Diagrams, 18b, 18c
Technology, 18c, 58b

LEARNING STRATEGIES

Assessment (Tests and skills checklists), 10d, 18d, 26d, 38d, 48d, 58d

Community Connections tasks, 48a

Culture sharing, 28, 38c, 60

Picture dictionary vocabulary lessons, 1, 11, 19, 29, 39, 49

Projects, 24

Grammar Index

Topic Index

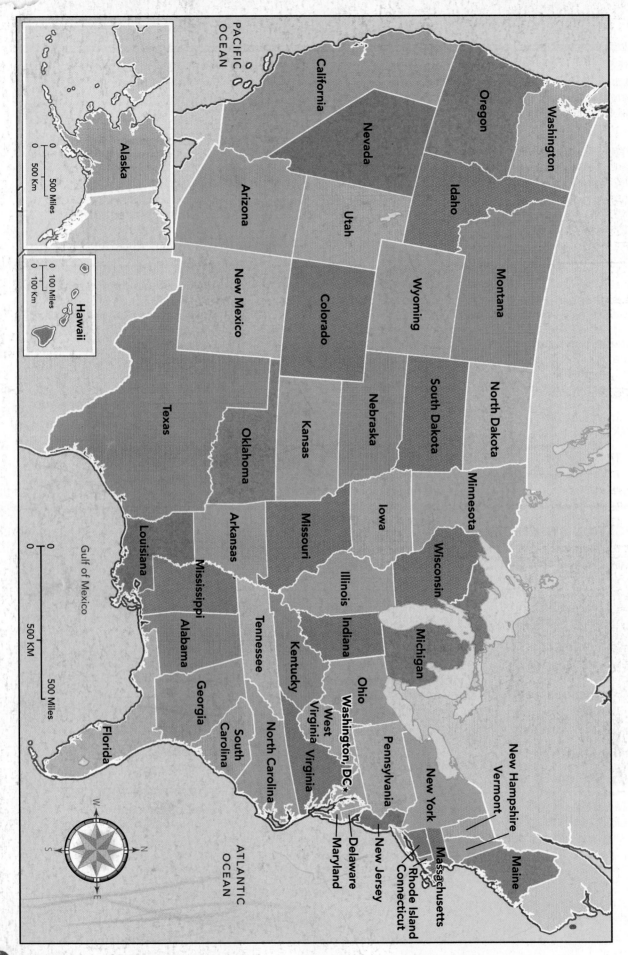

PACIFIC OCEAN

Alaska

0 500 Miles
0 500 Km

Hawaii

0 100 Miles
0 100 Km

Washington

Oregon

California

Nevada

Idaho

Montana

Arizona

Utah

Wyoming

New Mexico

Colorado

North Dakota

South Dakota

Nebraska

Kansas

Minnesota

Texas

Oklahoma

Iowa

Wisconsin

Arkansas

Missouri

Illinois

Indiana

Michigan

Louisiana

Mississippi

Alabama

Tennessee

Kentucky

Ohio

Washington, D.C.★

West Virginia

Virginia

Pennsylvania

New York

New Hampshire

Vermont

Maine

Georgia

South Carolina

North Carolina

Maryland

Delaware

New Jersey

Connecticut

Rhode Island

Massachusetts

Florida

Gulf of Mexico

0
0 500 KM
500 Miles

ATLANTIC OCEAN

W N S E